THE ATHEIST VIEWPOINT

THE ATHEIST VIEWPOINT

Advisory Editor:
Madalyn Murray O'Hair

THE

HISTORY OF THE LAST

TRIAL BY JURY FOR ATHEISM

IN ENGLAND

BY GEORGE JACOB HOLYOAKE.

ARNO PRESS & THE NEW YORK TIMES
New York / 1972

Reprint Edition 1972 by Arno Press Inc.

LC# 75-161331
ISBN 0-405-03792-9

The Atheist Viewpoint
ISBN for complete set: 0-405-03620-5
See last pages of this volume for titles.

Manufactured in the United States of America

THE

HISTORY OF THE LAST

TRIAL BY JURY FOR ATHEISM

IN ENGLAND:

A Fragment of Autobiography,

SUBMITTED FOR THE PERUSAL OF HER MAJESTY'S ATTORNEY-GENERAL
AND THE BRITISH CLERGY.

BY GEORGE JACOB HOLYOAKE.

> I was present in the court, to witness the trial of George Jacob Holyoake. I heard Wooler and Hone defend themselves successfully in 1817; but I would prefer to be declared guilty with Holyoake to being acquitted on the ground of Wooler and Hone.—RICHARD CARLILE.

[SECOND THOUSAND.]

LONDON:
JAMES WATSON, 3, QUEEN'S HEAD PASSAGE,
PATERNOSTER ROW.

1851.

TO

WILLIAM JOHN BIRCH, M.A.,

OF NEW INN HALL, OXON.,

IN WHOM FREE DISCUSSION HAS FOUND

AN ACCOMPLISHED DEFENDER AND MUNIFICENT FRIEND;

WHO WAS FIRST TO HELP US

WHEN A FRIEND IS TWICE A FRIEND,

WHEN WE WERE UNKNOWN AND STRUGGLING;

THIS HISTORY OF SIX MONTHS IMPRISONMENT

Is Inscribed,

BY

GEORGE JACOB HOLYOAKE.

PREFACE.

THE events, more than half of which are newly narrated in this 'History,' are recited from recollection. It is not pretended that all the conversations took place with the brevity with which they are given here. In the lapse of eight years there is much which I must have forgotten; but what I have told I distinctly remember, and the actors living will not, I think, contradict it

As, by a creditable improvement in English law, the recommencement of prosecutions for (ir)religious opinion can originate with the Attorney-General alone, I have ventured to hope that, if this narrative should fall into the hands of that officer for the time being, it may present some reasons to him why this 'Last Trial by Jury for Atheism' should be the *last*.

There are some passages in these Fragments over which some will be sad with me. Others will assume them to be written for effect; for such, let me say, they were not written at all. These pages will leave me for the press with much more pleasure if I can believe that no one will connect them with me, but read them as a posthumous record of bygone events. At times I thought I would omit all incidents of feeling; but I felt, that if I did so the narrative would not represent the whole (personal) truth of these proceedings—and, as they stand, they may serve to suggest to some a doubt of the correctness of the oft-repeated dictum of the Rev. Robert Hall, that ' Atheism is a bloody and a ferocious system, which finds nothing above us to excite awe, nor around us to awaken tenderness.'

Whether these are sufficient reasons for the purpose, I know not; but this I know—they are the true ones. As I very much dislike being an object of pity, those will much mistake me who suppose that this narrative has been written to excite it. In my estimation, imprisonment was a matter of conscience. I neither provoked prosecution nor shrank from it; and I am now as far from desiring it as I trust I ever shall be from fearing it. I do not pretend to despise public approval, but I think it should be regarded as a contingent reward, not as the sole motive of action; for he who only works while the public (always fickle in memory) care to remember him, is animated by a very precarious patriotism. As I have once before said, it is an encouragement to me that others may profit by any public principle I may assist in maintaining: but my interest in it is personal also. Though no one else desired freedom, it is enough for me that I desire it; and I would maintain the conflict for it, as best I could, though no one else cared about it ; and, as I choose to make the purchase, I do not higgle about the price. Tyranny has its soldiers, and why not Freedom? While thousands daily perish at the shrine of passion, what is the pain of a sacrifice now and then for public principle or personal freedom?

G. J. H.

THE HISTORY

OF THE

LAST TRIAL BY JURY FOR ATHEISM.

CHAPTER I.—BEFORE THE IMPRISONMENT.

THAT day is chilled in my memory when I first set out for Cheltenham. It was in December 1840. The snow had been frozen on the ground a fortnight. There were three of us, Mrs. Holyoake, Madeline (our first child), and myself. I had been residing in Worcester, which was the first station to which I had been appointed as a Social Missionary. My salary (16s. per week) was barely sufficient to keep us alive in summer. In winter it was inherent obstinacy alone which made us believe that we existed. I feel now the fierce blast which came in at the train windows from 'the fields of Tewkesbury,' on the day on which we travelled from Worcester to Cheltenham. The intense cold wrapped us round like a cloak of ice.

The shop lights threw their red glare over the snow-bedded ground as we entered the town of Cheltenham, and nothing but the drift and ourselves moved through the deserted streets. When at last we found a fire we had to wait to thaw before we could begin to speak. When tea was over we were escorted to the house where we were to stay for the night. I was told it was 'a friend's house.' Cheltenham is a fashionable town, a watering, visiting place, where everything is genteel and thin. As the parlours of some prudent house-wives are kept for show, and not to sit in, so in Cheltenham numerous houses are kept 'to be let,' and not to live in. The people who belong to the apartments are like the supernumeraries on a stage, they are employed in walking over them. Their clothes are decent—but they cannot properly be said to wear them: they carry them about with them (on their backs of course, because that mode is most convenient) but simply to show that they have such things. In the same manner eating and drinking is partly pantomime, and not a received reality. Such a house as I have suggested was the 'friend's house' to which we were conducted till lodgings could be found. We were asked to sit by the kitchen fire on 'the bench in the corner,' and there we sat from eight till one o'clock, without being asked to take anything to eat. Madeline, deprived of her usual rest, continued sucking at the breast till her mother was literally too exhausted to speak. A neighbouring festivity kept my 'friends' up that night till two o'clock—up to which time we saw no prospect of bed or supper. As we entered the house, Eleanor, with a woman's prescience, said 'George, you had better go and buy some food.' 'Buy food,' I replied, in simplicity, 'the people at this fine house will be outraged to see me bring in food.' Retribution was not far off. I repented me of my credulity that night. When at last I clearly comprehended that we were to have nothing to eat, I proceeded to take affairs into my own hands, and being too well assured of the insensibility of my host, I did it in a way that I conceived suited to his capacity, and began as follows :

'We have talked all night about social progress, and if you have no objection we will make some. And if eating,' I added, 'be not an irregular thing in your house, we will take some supper.'

'I am very sorry to say,' he answered, 'we have nothing to offer you.'

'Charge me bed and board while we are with you,' I rejoined, 'but let us have *both*. You have bread, I suppose?'

'We have some *rice* bread.'

'Perhaps you will toast it.'

'Will you have it *toasted*?'

'I will. Could you not make coffee?'

'We have no coffee.'

'Tea?'

'We have no tea.'

'Any water?'

'No *hot* water.'

'Any butter?'

'Yes, we have *salt* butter.'

'Then put some on the bread,' I added, for he did not even propose to do that. I had to dispute every inch of hospitality with him. My 'friend,' Mr. V., was an instance of that misplacement of which Plato speaks in his 'Republic.' What a capital Conservative he would have made! No innovation with him—not even into his own loaf! I was obliged to take the initiative into the 'salt' butter.

After seeing the bread toasted, and buttering it myself, to make sure that it was buttered, I put on my hat and went into the streets, in search of material out of which to manufacture a cordial, for eight hours had then elapsed since Eleanor had had any sustenance, and my good host's choice reserve of cold water did not seem quite adequate to revive her.

When I reached the dark streets, to which I was so absolute a stranger, not knowing where I stood on the slippery ground, made so by frozen rain on a bedding of snow, I had not gone (or rather *slipped*) far before I was fairly lost. Like the sense in a Rousseauian love-letter, I neither knew whence I came nor whither I was going, and when I succeeded in my errand it was at the last place at which I should wish to be found.

During my absence that voluptuous caterer, 'mine host,' whom I had left behind—whose counterpart Maginn must have had before him when he drew the portrait of ' Quarantotti'—had proceeded so far as to boil some water. The evening ended without inconsistency, and the bed corresponded with the supper.

The next day I took lodgings, where, expecting nothing, I was no longer disappointed. But on this occasion, profiting by the experience of the preceding night, I went provided with a small stock of loaves and chocolate. My stay in Cheltenham was more agreeable than was to be expected after such an introduction; but I remember that I had to pay my expenses back again, and though they only amounted to 12s., I felt the want of them for a long time afterwards. Yet Cheltenham was not without generous partizans, but, as is common in the incipiency of opinion, they were at that time among that class who had fewest means. The experience here recounted was a sample of that frequently recurring, but not exactly of the kind on which vanity is nurtured, as the reader will think as he reverts (from a speech to be recited) to these incidents. He who reads thus far will acquit me of any premeditation of disturbing the peace of the religious inhabitants of Cheltenham, for it is certainly the last town I should have selected as the scene of such an occurrence as the one which I have to narrate.

My next location was in a northern manufacturing town, where I was treated like its iron-ware — case hardened. My salary there of 30s. per week was a subject of frequent discussion by the members of the Branch. For this sum I taught a Day School and lectured on Sunday. And as he who lives the life of a child all the week (as he must do who teaches children to any purpose) finds it hard to live that of a man on Sunday, my duties were wearying and perplexing. Those who grudged my salary made no sufficient allowance for that application necessary for the discharge of my duties—an application which often commenced long before they were up in the morning, and continued long after their mechanical employment was over at night. Not comprehending myself, at that time, that they who work for the improvement of others must not calculate on their appreciation as an encouragement, but as a *result*, I was thrown into that unpleasant state in which my pride incited me to stop and my duty to go on. It was not till subsequent to my return from Glasgow, four years afterwards, that I mastered the problem thus raised which so many have been ruined in solving. Though an Anti-Priest, my treatment was that of a priest. My congregation, as is the case with most Freethinkers, objected to the pay of the priest, when the true quarrel was with error, and not with payment: for if a man has the truth, it is well that it should be his interest to hold it. But Dissent, objecting to the pay of others, has been left without pay itself—hence its apostles have been reduced to fight the lowest battles of animal wants, when they should have been fighting for the truth. Dissent has too often paid its advocates the bad compliment of supposing, that if placed within reach of competence they would either fall into indolence or hypocrisy. It has acted practically upon the hypothesis, that the only possible way of ensuring their zeal and sincerity was to starve them—a policy which leaves progress to the mercy of accident. For a long period the operation of this policy chilled me. My initiation into affairs of progress was in company with men who estimated, above all other virtues, the virtue which worked for nothing. They would denounce the patriotism of that man who accepted a shilling for making a speech, although it had cost him more to compose it than those who heard it would probably give to save their country. Nine tenths of the best public men and women I have known, have turned back at this point. Not any new conviction—not any bribe of the enemy, but the natural though unwise revolt against being considered mendicants, has forced them back into supineness, indifference, or even into the very ranks of oppression. True, I felt that he who labours with his brains is worthy of his hire as well as he who labours with his hands. As often as I read a book or heard a lecture, which threw new light on the paths of life, I found that it not only relieved me from the dominion of ignorance, but imparted to me the strength of intelligence. I felt indebted to the author and speaker, for I found that knowledge was not only *power*, but *property*. I knew all this, but painful years passed over me before I acquired the courage to offer what instruction I had to impart as an article of commercial value. Those who have encountered this kind of experience know that the feeling it engenders is one of indifference, and that an unusual speech would arise in a cold sense of duty, and not in wantonness or wickedness. Thus much will inform the reader of the circumstances under which I spoke the alleged blasphemy in Cheltenham.

A fellow-missionary, Mr. Charles Southwell, had, in conjunction with Mr. Chilton and Mr. Field, set up an Atheistical periodical in Bristol, entitled the *Oracle of Reason*—which the authorities attempting forcibly to put down, Mr. Southwell was sentenced to twelve months' imprisonment in Bristol Gaol. On a visit to him I walked ninety miles from Birmingham to Bristol, and as my way lay through Cheltenham, I staid a night in that town to deliver a lecture on 'Home Colonisation as a means of superseding Poor Laws and Emigration.' At the conclusion of the lecture I instructed the chairman to make the announcement, which I still make after my lectures, viz., that any of the audience may put relevant questions or offer what objections they consider useful—whereupon a person stood up of the name of Maitland, a teetotaller, and sort of local preacher, and complained that 'though I had told them their duty to man, I had not told them of their duty to God,' and inquired 'whether we should have churches and chapels in community?'

I answered thus: 'I do not desire to have religion mixed up with an economical and secular subject, but as Mr. Maitland has introduced questions in reference to religion I will answer him frankly. Our national debt already hangs like a millstone round the poor man's neck, and our national church and general religious institutions cost us, upon accredited computation, about twenty millions annually. Worship being thus expensive, I appeal to your heads and your pockets whether we are not too poor to have a God? If poor men cost the state as much, they would be put like officers upon half-pay, and while our distress lasts I think it would be wise to do the same thing with deity. Thus far I object, as a matter of political economy, to build chapels in communities. If others want them they have themselves to please, but I, not being religious, cannot propose them. Morality I regard, but I do not believe there is such a thing as a God.* The pulpit says "Search the Scriptures," and they who are thus trepanned get imprisoned in Bristol jail, like my friend Mr. Southwell. For myself, I flee the Bible as a viper, and revolt at the touch of a Christian.'

Perhaps this reply was indecorous, but it was nothing more, and as it was delivered in a tone of conversational freedom, it produced only quiet amusement on the meeting. The next day I continued my journey to Bristol. A day or two after I received the *Cheltenham Chronicle*, commonly called the Rev. Francis Close's paper, it being the organ of his party, in which I read the following paragraph—written with that exaggerated virulence which Archdeacon Hare has subsequently deprecated as the bane of religious journalism, but which at that time was considered as a holy ornament:—

* I do not remember using this phrase, but as the witnesses reported it perhaps it was so; but I still incline to the opinion that it was an expression they fell upon in stating their impressions of the meeting to their employers, and all working in one office, they fell into one story, either through inadvertence or from precaution.

ATHEISM AND BLASPHEMY.—On Tuesday evening last a person named Holyoake, from Sheffield, (?) delivered a lecture on Socialism (or, as it has been more appropriately termed, devilism), at the Mechanics' Institution. After attacking the Church of England and religion generally for a considerable time, he said he was open to any question that might be put to him. A teetotaller named Maitland then got up, and said the lecturer had been talking a good deal about our duty to man, but he omitted to mention our duty towards God, and he would be glad to know if there were any chapels in the community? The Socialist then replied that he professed no religion at all, and thought they were too poor to have any. He did not believe there was such a being as a God, and impiously remarked that *if there was,** he would have the deity served the same as government treated the subalterns, by placing him upon half-pay. With many similar blasphemous and awful remarks, which we cannot sully our columns by repeating, the poor misguided wretch continued to address the audience. To their lasting shame, be it spoken, a considerable portion of the company applauded the miscreant during the time he was giving utterance to these profane opinions.

[We have three persons in our employ who are ready to verify on oath the correctness of the above statements. We therefore hope those in authority will not suffer the matter to rest here, but that some steps will immediately be taken to prevent any further publicity to such diabolical sentiments.— ED. *Cheltenham Chronicle*.]

Some have censured the openness of my answer to Mr. Maitland as being inexpedient. It is not impossible to justify it on that ground, but I have an aversion to do it. Expediency has nothing to do with what a man shall say. Expediency may close the mouth, but it has no power over the speech if the mouth once opens. A man may keep silence if he chooses, but if he does speak he has no alternative but to speak that which is frank and true. But at that time there were political reasons why I should not evade the question put to me. The *Odd-Fellow* of Mr. Hetherington (under the editorship of W. J. Linton) had shortly before contained an able article beginning thus:—

The world need not be much frightened at the present race of Socialists. However heinous their doctrines may be thought, there need be no fear; they will not act in too close accordance with them. For ourselves, having been among them at various times, we have never yet been able to discover any certain marks, whether of manner, of opinion, or of conduct, whereby to distinguish them from the mass of professing Christians. However heterodox their innermost sentiments, they usually maintain as decent an appearance of conformity with custom as the most worldly and orthodox could desire.

This was a character which no progressive party could live with, and as the hypocrisy here charged upon us was generally believed, and not wholly without reason, it became necessary either to give up the party or refute the accusation. The attack on Mr. Owen's friends, by the Bishop of Exeter in the House of Lords, had been evaded, not met, and a noble opportunity, such as bigotry seldom affords to a rising party, had been suffered to pass away unused. The enemy triumphed. In this very town of

---

* This is an interpolation.

Cheltenham a young poet, named Sperry, who betrayed freethinking tendencies, had been called upon to recant. He did so, and then he was treated with contempt by those who intimidated him. They first destroyed his moral influence, and then despised him. I had therefore sufficient public reasons for not tempting a similar fate. If I had refused to reply, it would have been said I held opinions too horrible to avow. Had I evaded the answer I should have been considered a time-server, and if I answered frankly there were the legal consequences in prospect. I was not very much skilled in policy, but I knew this much, that when a man cannot take care of consequences, he ought to take care of the credit of his cause. A little anticipating this history I may say that the expediency of the course I took, if the expediency must be defended, was shown in the altered tone of the authorities, both in Cheltenham and Gloucester, after my trial. Instead of that contempt with which persons holding Socialist opinions are treated, there was a somewhat respectful recognition of them. However crude might be considered my defence of my views, nothing escaped me that could be distorted into a willingness to avoid any suffering at the expense of my adherence to the principles I had adopted. Many persons, who would not have spoken to me before, came and expressed regret at what had happened, and I met with many instances of regard from persons who had formerly despised those with whom I acted.

I was indebted to the *Odd-Fellow* of July 23, then edited by Eben Jones, author of 'Studies of Sensation and Event,' for the fairest statement of my conduct and of the point in question, which the press gave. It was thus expressed:—

We cannot refrain from saying, that under the peculiar circumstances, Mr. Holyoake (presuming his disbelief in a God to be sincere) could not have said other than he did say, and at the same time have continued honest. It is true he was not asked, 'Do you believe in a God?' but a question was put to him which assumed his belief in a God, and had he not testified at once his disbelief, he would have sanctioned the false assumption : and if not a liar, would have been at least the permitter of a lie ; between which is no distinction recognised by an honourable man. In arguing thus we would not express any sympathy whatever with Mr. Holyoake's atheism, we are merely concerned to show that it was not Mr. Holyoake's right alone, but absolutely his DUTY, to say that 'he did not believe in a God.' It was his duty, if it be the duty of man to be honest ; he could not have spoken otherwise, unless he had 'lied against his heart,' and lied towards mankind.

The next number of the aforesaid *Cheltenham Chronicle* brought me this further notice:—

HOLYOAKE THE BLASPHEMOUS SOCIALIST LECTURER.—In reference to a paragraph which appeared in the last *Chronicle* regarding this monster, the magistrates read the article alluded to, and expressed their opinion that it was a clear case of blasphemy. In order to check the further progress of his pernicious doctrines, the superintendent of police was ordered to use every exertion to bring him to justice.

On reading this paragraph I lost no time in setting out for Cheltenham, to hold a public meeting and justify myself to the town. Foot-sore and weary—for the journey was more than thirty miles, and the day very hot—I reached Cheltenham on the 1st of June, and proceeded as privately as a 'monster' could to my friends the Adamses. The next night I slid like sleep into the meeting, lest the police should prevent me from addressing it. Mr. Leech, a leading Chartist, presided, and the meeting was addressed by Messrs. Parker, jun., Geo. Adams, W. Bilson, and J. B. Lear. The Chartists of Cheltenham at that time held possession of the Mechanics' Institution, and they were threatened with the loss of it, if they let it to me to speak in any more. But as I required it in self-defence they generously disregarded the menace, and permitted me the use of it. My friends in the distant town of Newcastle-upon-Tyne afterwards gracefully acknowledged this kindness by making a collection for Mrs. Holberry, the wife of a Sheffield Chartist who had perished in prison. Before I had been long in the meeting, Superintendent Russell came in with about a dozen men, who were arranged on each side the door, and their glazed hats formed a brilliant, but a dubious back ground for a meeting on Free-Discussion. I spoke an hour after they came in. So rare an audience was not to be thrown away, and I thought we might convert some of them. At the conclusion Superintendent Russell, who had the politeness to wait till we had done, intimated that he had instructions to apprehend me. I asked for his warrant. He said he had none. It was in vain that I protested against the irregularity of the proceeding. He replied that his instructions were imperative upon him—and it was thereupon arranged that I should walk down to the station with Mr. Hollis, a well-known gun maker of Cheltenham, and there, the meeting following, we arrived in procession between eleven and twelve o'clock.

To the truth, it is no great proof *à posteriori* of a man's extravagance, that he should be involved in legal proceedings in Cheltenham on account of freedom of speech. Owing to priestly and conventional influences, that town will furnish a jury who would, under direction, bring in any man guilty of blasphemy who boiled his tea-kettle on a Sunday. Not long before the time now spoken of, a Mormon preacher, holding forth there, happened to say that the Elements of Euclid were as true as the Bible : and for this he was indicted for blasphemy, and was only saved from imprisonment by the grand jury (who must have had infidel tendencies) throwing out the bill.

On the morning after my apprehension I was taken before the Rev. Dr. Newell, R. Capper, and J. Overbury, Esquires, magistrates of Cheltenham. The Rev. Dr. Newell ought to have had the pride, if not the decency, to have kept away.

The *Cheltenham Chronicle* reported that ' George Jacob Holyoake, who was described as a Socialist lecturer, and as the editor of the *Oracle of Reason*, was charged with delivering atheistical and blasphemous sentiments at the Mechanics' Institution, on the evening of the 24th of May. The prisoner had been apprehended last night, after delivering another lecture at the same place. The affair appeared to have caused great sensation, and several persons attended at the office anxious to hear the examination. Amongst the number were some individuals who, without the blush of shame mantling their cheeks, acknowledged themselves friends of the accused.'

Mr. Bubb, a local solicitor, a particularly gross and furious man, then said—' I attend to prefer the charge of blasphemy, and I shall take my stand on the common unwritten law of the land. There have been a variety of statutes passed for punishing blasphemy, but these statutes in no way interfere with the common unwritten law. (Mr. Capper nodded assent.)* Any person who denies the existence or providence of God is guilty of blasphemy, and the law has annexed to that offence imprisonment, corporal punishment, and fine. I shall give evidence of the facts, and I shall ask that he be committed for trial, or required to find bail for his appearance. The offence is much aggravated by his having put forth a placard, announcing a lecture on a subject completely innocent, and having got together a number of persons, has given utterance to those sentiments which are an insult to God and man.'

The assertion that I had employed duplicity in choosing my subject was quite gratuitous. Addressing the Bench, I asked whether it was legal in these cases to apprehend persons without the authority of a warrant?

Mr. Capper replied, ' Any person in the meeting would be justified in taking you up without the authority of a warrant,' which showed that the Bench were better read in Bigotry than in Blackstone. I said it was customary in other towns, where bigotry existed to a greater degree even than it did there, for information to be laid and a regular notice served.

Mr. Capper said, ' We refuse to hold an argument with a man professing the abominable principle of denying the existence of a Supreme Being.' This was not a very legal way of getting rid of my objections, but it answered in Cheltenham.

Two witnesses, James Bartram and William Henry Pearce,

* Mr. Bubb took his stand on the common law because his object was to make it a *sessions* case, and to take it out of the statutary law, which (9 & 10 Will. 3, c. 32) would have required that information of the words spoken should be laid before a justice of the peace within four days from their utterance, and would likewise have implied a trial at the *assizes*.

both of the *Chronicle* office, were adduced to report the words that formed the ground of the indictment. Neither of them could recollect anything else but the objectionable words reported in their own paper, and to these they did not swear positively, but only to the 'best of their belief.' Mr. Pearce was not produced at the trial at the Assizes, he having no local reputation but that of a dog-fancier and fighter, which did not render him a creditable authority on matters pertaining to religion. Bartram's sister was a Socialist, and she came to me some years after, in Manchester, to apologise for the disgrace brought upon her family by the weakness or the ignorance of her brother.

Mr. Overbury said he considered the case satisfactorily proved, and added, 'Whether you are of no religion *is of very little consequence to us*, but your attempt to propagate the infamous sentiment that there is no God, is calculated to produce disorder and confusion, and is a breach of the peace.' This was the remark of an ill-informed politician rather than of a Christian.

Being required to enter into my own recognizances of £100, and find two sureties of £50 each, Mr. Partridge became one, and Mr. Henry Fry, editor of the *Educational Circular*, offered himself as the other. But the Rev. Dr. Newell objected to Mr. Fry's bail, on the ground that he did not swear positively that he was worth £50 when all his debts were paid. He swore only that 'to the best of his belief' he was so. I reminded the Bench that they had accepted the evidence of the witnesses against me on the same ground, namely 'the best of their belief.' Hereupon the Rev. Dr. Newell, with an air of outraged morality, exclaimed 'Come, come! we'll have no quibbling.'

I answered that I did not propose to quibble, for if that had been to my taste I might have avoided standing there at that moment. Mr. Bubb then interjected that he should demand twenty-four hours' notice of bail. Another gentleman then offered himself, whom I desired to sit down and let the Bench take their own course. This indifference with regard to the Bench incensed them very much.

Mr. Capper said, 'Even the heathens acknowledged the existence of a Deity. If you entertain the same pernicious opinion on your death-bed you will be a bold man indeed. But you are only actuated by a love of notoriety.' I only answered, 'Why do you address me thus, since you will not allow me to reply?' and I turned away repeating to myself the words of Sir Thomas Browne —'There is a rabble amongst the gentry as well as the commonalty; a sort of plebeian heads, whose fancy moves with the same wheel as these: men in the same level with mechanics, though their fortunes do somewhat gild their infirmities, and their purses compound for their follies.'

But I ought to say that during these proceedings the people in the court, of juster feeling than the magistrates, frequently expressed their disapprobation of the speeches made to me.

Mr. Capper's assertion that I was only actuated by a love of notoriety, were just the words to do me injury. The respectable people near, and the intelligent people at a distance, would believe the magistrate and disbelieve the sceptic, who had no friends to rebut the imputation. The vulgar bearing of this brutal old man lingered long in my memory as the most distinct thing of these proceedings. I should have thought less of it had it not come from an old man. The aged always inspire me with reverence, in their kindly aspects. They are the links which nature perpetuates between old time and our time—the human chroniclers of an experience the young can never know. They have followed the hearse of the old world, and are the legatees of Time, who has bequeathed to them his secrets and his conquests, which they in their turn distribute to us. When living at Islington, in 1848, I frequently passed, but not without sadness, nor sometimes without tears, an old man who stood near the Merlin's Cave to beg. He resembled one whom I cannot name. I could see on his brow the fresh traces of a struggle still going on between dignity and destitution. And I often gave him the price of the biscuit intended for my dinner, in the secret hope we all have in a kind act that some one else may repeat it to those we love ; and I indulged the hope that others might approach with the same respectful feelings him to whom I have alluded, if ever, with untamed pride and broken heart, he should stand in his grey hairs on the high way to beg—which I have dreaded through so many years.

When taken back to the station-house, Captain Lefroy, who was at the head of the police, introduced me to Mr. Pinching, surgeon of the same corps. The captain, in a gentlemanly way, inquired if I would allow Mr. Pinching to reason with me on my opinions ? I said, 'Certainly.' Mr. Pinching asked me the irrelevant question ' Did I believe in Jesus Christ ?' and began a dry, historical argument to prove that there was the same evidence for the existence of Jesus Christ as for that of Henry the Fourth. I said, ' The argument is unnecessary with me. I do not care to argue whether he existed or not. My inquiry is not whether he lived, but what he *said*.' Mr. Pinching's next speech was delivered with an air of sharp authority, and he began to address me rather rudely.

He asked me was it not Robert Owen who made me an atheist ? I replied, Mr. Owen himself was not an atheist. For myself, I had not become so till after the imprisonment of Mr. Southwell, which had led me to inquire into the grounds of religious opinion more closely than I had before done, and it had ended in my entire disbelief.

Mr. Pinching now became impatient and abusive, allowing me no opportunity of replying, and I said 'Stop! stop! sir, you must not treat me as a prisoner if you intend me to hear you. Unless you converse with me upon equal terms I shall not answer you.' Lefroy laughed, and said, 'Come! come! Pinching, I think you are not quite fair.' After this Mr. Pinching became more abusive, and I turned away—when he ended the conversation by saying, 'I am only sorry the day is gone by when we could send you and Owen of Lanark to the stake instead of to Gloucester gaol.'

Not allowed to wait twenty-four hours to see if I could obtain bail, I was soon after sent off to Gloucester, nine miles away, the same afternoon, where the difficulty of negotiating my release was so much increased that it took me a fortnight to do it.

After my conversation with Mr. Pinching I was shut up in a very filthy place with a lousy man. I was handcuffed with small old irons that pinched my wrists, and I begged to have another pair of handcuffs put on, which was done: then I was made to walk through Cheltenham town and suburbs, and afterwards through Gloucester city, with the hand irons on. As I had walked thirty miles to be apprehended, they had no reason to suspect me of making my escape; nor was it customary to handcuff prisoners conveyed to Gloucester on foot. In my case it was done to pain and degrade me.

A memorial of a public meeting, sent from the town of Cheltenham to the House of Commons, on this subject, stated 'That notwithstanding Mr. Holyoake offered no resistance to any officer or procedure, and was at the same time in very delicate health and much exhausted, yet it was deemed necessary to lock both his hands in irons and make him walk to Gloucester—a distance of near nine miles—on a most sultry day, but on the way thither his friends interfered and obtained leave for him to ride, on condition only that they should pay his expenses as well as the expenses of two policemen to accompany him.' And it may be added that though I sat an hour at the station, waiting for the train, my hands were not unlocked.

The same memorial also alleged 'That the conduct of the magistrates during the proceedings indicated a predisposition to punish Mr. Holyoake, independently of any evidence which he might have offered in defence of his own conduct.'

The Member for Bath, to whom this memorial was entrusted, paid to it the most generous attention, and immediately returned the following reply:—

London, June 23rd, 1842.

Sir,—The petition you sent me is of a nature that demands serious inquiry, and I thought I should best discharge my duty towards the petitioners and Mr. Holyoake by at once addressing myself to Sir James Graham. He has very promptly taken up the inquiry, and I have no doubt but that substantial justice will be done. If, however, the petitioners should hereafter deem that justice has not been done, I can present their petition after the inquiry which has been undertaken by the Home Secretary has been closed. I have taken this liberty with the petition on my own responsibility, hoping that the petitioners will here trust to my discretion, and they for the moment will put confidence in my judgment. I will write you word so soon as I hear from the Home Secretary, who has now the petition in his hands for the purpose of immediately instituting a searching inquiry.

I am, sir, your obedient servant,

Mr. H. Fry. J. A. ROEBUCK.

The committal the police bore with them was to the following effect:—

[GLOUCESTERSHIRE TO WIT.]—To all and every of the constables and other officers of the peace for the said county, and to the keeper of the gaol at Gloucester in the said county—

WHEREAS George Jacob Holyoake is now brought before us, three of Her Majesty's Justices of the Peace in and for the said county, and charged, on the oaths of James Bartram and William Henry Pearce, with having, on the twenty-fourth day of May last, at the parish of Cheltenham in the said county, *wickedly* and profanely uttered, made use of, and proclaimed, in the presence of a public assembly of men, women, and children, then and there assembled, certain impious and blasphemous words against God, and of and concerning the Christian religion, to wit, 'That he was of no religion at all,' and 'that he did not believe there was such a thing as a God,' and that if he could have his way he would place the Deity on half-pay, as the government of this country did the subaltern officers,' *against the peace of our lady the Queen, her crown and dignity*. And whereas we, the said justices, have required the said George Jacob Holyoake to become bound in the sum of one hundred pounds, and to find two sufficient sureties in the sum of fifty pounds each, conditioned for the appearance of the said George Jacob Holyoake at the next Quarter Sessions of the peace, to be holden at Gloucester, in and for the said county, and then and there to answer to any bill of indictment that may be preferred against him for his said offence, which he hath neglected to do,

These are therefore in Her Majesty's name to command you, and every of you the said constables, forthwith safely to convey and deliver into the custody of the keeper of the said gaol the body of the said George Jacob Holyoake.

And you, the said keeper, are hereby required to receive the said George Jacob Holyoake into your said custody, and him safely keep until the said next general Quarter Sessions of the peace, to be holden at Gloucester, in and for the said county, or until he become bound and finds such sureties as aforesaid, or until he shall be thence delivered by due course of law. And for your so doing this shall be to you and every of you a sufficient warrant.

Given under our hands and seals the third day of June, in the year of our Lord One Thousand Eight Hundred and Forty-two.

ROBT. CAPPER,
J. B. NEWELL,
JOSEPH OVERBURY.

Twenty-four hours' notice of bail to be given.

I hereby certify that the above is a true copy of a warrant, by virtue of which the within named George Jacob Holyoake was brought into custody the 3rd day of June, 1842. Witness my hand,

THOMAS MOORE,
Clerk to the county gaol of Gloucester.

Some of the magistrates characterised the speech for which I was committed as 'Felony,' 'a breach of the peace,' etc., and I was told that my committal was made out for 'felony.' Serious comments were made thereupon by the public. Able strictures on the subject were made by 'Philo Publicola,' in the *Weekly Dispatch*. But the magistrates grew wiser as they grew cooler, and on the copy of the committal subsequently furnished to me, the charge of felony did not appear.

A very curious circumstance deserves mentioning here. The magistrates being censured in the House of Commons for their 'irregularities' in my case (as will be explained in my defence further on) an attempt was made to fix the blame on Mr. Russell, superintendent of the police. This induced me to address the following letter to the editor of the *Cheltenham Free Press*:—

SIR,—Observing an attempt has been made in Parliament by the Hon. Craven Berkley to fix the blame of my 'harsh treatment' on the constables of your town, and to implicate Superintendent Russell, I beg to say that after my committal I never saw Mr. Russell, and never once said, or suspected, that the harshness exercised towards me, while ostensibly in his custody, originated with him. His courtesy to me on the night of my apprehension, of which I retain a lively sense, forbids such a conclusion.

I shall be glad if you will insert this in your next number. I can never consent to purchase public sympathy by a silence which may unjustly sacrifice any person's interest. I was justified in making the complaints I have, but would rather they were for ever unredressed than that an innocent man should suffer.

Birmingham, July 30, 1842. G. JACOB HOLYOAKE.

Soon after Mr. Russell left the corps, and appears to have been offered up by the magistrates as a sacrifice for the irregularities *they* had committed.

On my arrival my pockets were searched, and even my pocketbook and letters taken from me. This I felt not only as an indignity, but also as a breach of faith. Before leaving Cheltenham, and when in communication with my friends, I inquired if my papers would be taken from me at Gloucester, and the officers answered 'No,' (but they must have known differently). Trusting their answer, however, I brought with me papers I should not otherwise have brought. Perhaps I was fevered after my walk, but the cell I was put into gave me a new sense. There had been times when I had wished for a sixth sense, but this was not the sense I coveted, for it was a sense of suffocation. The bed was so filthy that I could not lie down, and sat on the side all night. When taken into the general room next morning the prisoners surrounded me, exclaiming, 'What are ye come for?' As I made no reply, another observed, 'We always tells one another.' 'Oh! blasphemy,' I replied. 'What's that?' said one. 'Aren't you 'ligious?' said another.

But as these rustics were happily unacquainted with doctrinal piety, they said nothing rude ; and seeing my loaf unbroken, and that I could not eat, 'Here,' said four or five at once, 'will you have some of this tea, zir ?'—which was mint-tea, the reward o some extra work, and the nicest thing they had to offer.

When the chaplain of the gaol, the Rev. Robert Cooper, came to see me, I told him that before I took anything from him for my soul, I wanted something from him for my defence; and I demanded my note book and papers. Mr. Samuel Jones, a visiting magistrate, brought me a few pencil notes which I had made during my examination in Cheltenham and some private papers, but he withheld many others relating to matters of opinion, saying that *he* ' did not think them necessary to my defence.' The clergyman has a veto on all books admitted, and of a list which I gave him, which I wanted to read for my trial, he only allowed me thirteen. He said the others ' were of an unchristian character,' and he could not let me have them.* I told him I was not going to make an orthodox defence. He would not relax, so I would not have any spiritual consolation, and we lived on very indifferent terms.

One day Mr. Bransby Cooper, and Mr. Samuel Jones (just mentioned), both old magistrates, came to visit me. Mr. Jones, I was told, had at one time been a preacher among the Methodists. He told me he would be kind to me, but all his kindness was religious kindness—the worst kindness I have ever experienced. I was then the sole occupant of the Queen's evidence side of the prison, a place I had chosen as I preferred to be alone. I had a large yard and all the cells to myself. In this solitary place these magistrates visited me. After teazing me with Leslie for a long time, Mr. Bransby Cooper concluded thus— ' Now! Holyoake, you are a Deist—are you not ?' I shook my head. ' You cannot be an atheist,' he continued, ' you don't look like one.' He said this, I suppose, seeing no horns on my head, and no eyes on my elbows, as he expected I answered that I felt very unpleasantly how much I was in their power, and had therefore some reason to desire to oblige them. Though sorry to say what might outrage them or look like obstinacy, yet out of respect to my own conscience I must say that I *was* an atheist. Upon these they both flew into indignant revulsions, and shouted

* See Report of Gloucester Trinity Sessions in the county papers of that period.

'a fool! a fool!' till the roof rang. Capt. Mason (the governor), who accompanied them, turned away a few paces, with the air of one not caring to be witness of so much rudeness.

Before leaving they said of course I should employ counsel to defend me. I answered, 'No, I should defend myself as well as I was able. Barristers were not good at stating a case of conscience.' They urged, they even coaxed me to abandon the idea of defending myself; but finding me not to be deterred, they threatened me that it would aggravate my case—reminded me of Hone and others, and said that the judge would put me down and not hear me. This menace, as will be seen hereafter, did me great harm. They reported my determination at the Trinity Sessions as though it was a matter desirable to be averted.

Mr. Bransby Cooper was a brother of Sir Astley Cooper. He was formerly member for Gloucester, and when he suspected that I did not regard his dignity sufficiently, he would slide in some remark about 'his friend' Sir James Graham, who was then Secretary of State for the Home Department. Bransby Cooper was the senior magistrate at this time—a man of venerable and commanding aspect, generous to a fault in matters of humanity, harsh to a fault in matters of religion. On his way through the city, old women would way-lay him to beg. First raising his stick against them—then threatening to commit them as vagrants—they fled from him in mock terror, but knowing the generous feelings of the man they returned again, and before he reached home he would empty his pockets among them. One minute he would growl at me like an unchained tiger—the next he would utter some word of real sympathy, such as came from no one else, and at the end of my imprisonment I parted from him with something of regret. He had the voice of Stentor, and though at first his savage roar shook me, at last I acquired an artistic liking for it, and his voice was so grand that I came to the conclusion that he had a natural right to be a brute. The old man, after his fashion, laboured very hard for my conversion. His son Robert was chaplain of the gaol, and had I happily been brought over, the old man would have given the credit to his boy. My conversion was thus a sort of family speculation.

Those who sent me to prison in default of bail, took care to make bail impossible to me by intimidating those who would have become my sureties, and after two weeks' anxiety I was obliged to accept the generous offer of two friends in Worcester—James Barnes and John Dymond Stevenson—to come from that city and enter into recognizances for me, and I was indebted to them for my liberation, after sixteen days' imprisonment.

So near was my trial upon my release that I had to return to

Gloucester within a fortnight. A great desire of my youth had been to see London. When I found myself suddenly shut up in gaol, in prospect of an indefinite term of imprisonment, which in my then state of health might prove fatal, my sole remorse was that I had never seen that city of my dreams. Once again at liberty I made a short visit to my family in Birmingham, and the next week found me in London.

Chafed and sad, with tremulous heart and irresolute step, it seems but yesterday that I walked through Woburn Place into the city in which I now write. Its streets, its pride, its magnificence enthralled me, and its very poverty fascinated me because nearer to my destiny. Savage and Johnson had walked those squares houseless, and why not I. Chatterton had perished in a garret, and garrets had something sacred in them. Solitary in that two million multitude, I was hardly known to any one in it, yet when I remembered that I was in London I felt an enchanted gladness, and in all vicissitudes of fortune and chequered struggles with fate, I have walked its magical streets with undimmed joy, and it is to me still a fairy land, whose atmosphere of enchantment feels as if it would never leave me.

How sweetly, how gratefully to me (as words never read before) came the notice the *Weekly Dispatch* gave of my first lecture in London. All the night before I had sat up with Ryall, answering correspondence and concerting my defence. When I reached the Rotunda it was more fitting that I should have found a bed there than a rostrum, for when I rose to speak I was weak as well as timid. To succeed in any way in London was more than I ventured to expect, and the nature of the report in the *Weekly Dispatch* inspired me with the hope of at least being tolerated.

I hastened back to Gloucester. Either a Secretary of State's order, or a Bill had come into operation, I was never correctly informed which, removing my trial from the Sessions to the Assizes, which gave me an impartial Judge to determine my case. At a Sessions' trial the parties who had caused my imprisonment, and the magistrates who had shown themselves my personal opponents, would have sat on the Bench to try me. Though unable to proceed with my trial after having committed me, they put me to the expense of bringing my bail from Worcester, and charged me £1 9s. for renewing my sureties.

My arrest caused a demand for atheistical publications in Cheltenham, which Mr. George Adams, partly as a friend to the free publication of opinion and partly from personal friendship to me, undertook to supply. In this he was joined by his wife, Harriet Adams, a very interesting and courageous woman.

On Monday evening, June 13th, at a public meeting called to consider the grounds of my own apprehension, Mr. George Adams was arrested for selling No. 25 of the *Oracle*, and forthwith conveyed to the station-house. As soon as a knowledge of the arrest came to the ears of Mrs. Adams, she went to the station-house to see her husband, when she, likewise, was served with a warrant for selling No. 4. Mrs. Adams says, (the account cannot be better rendered than in her own words) ' I went to see my husband at the station-house, when I was detained; a policeman was sent home with me to fetch my infant, and I had to leave four at home in bed. The man that went with me to the station was a rude fellow; he was quite abusive to me, telling me I should be locked up from my husband; saying, it was quite time such things were put a stop to. When we arrived at the station-house he would have locked me in a cell with drunken women, had I not sat down in the yard and insisted on seeing the superintendent, who then allowed me to sit up in a kitchen, where policemen were coming in and out all night. My husband was much troubled on my account.' The four children were left locked up in the house alone.

Mr. Bubb's speech, when Adams was brought up, is so curious a relic of provincial barbarism that I preserve it, or those who are told of it in time to come will regard the story as some malicious fiction Mr. Bubb opened the charge by justifying himself and clients—' It has been said that we are prosecuting here for the entertaining of opinions merely. That proposition I deny. The entertaining of opinions is not opposed to law if people keep them to themselves. If they step out of the way, and seek to propagate them by undermining the institutions of the country, by denying the existence of a God, by robbing others of " the hopes set before them," without offering the flimsiest pretext, it is the duty of all to prevent this. Such is the opinion of those gentlemen who set on foot these proceedings, and no clamour of persecution will prevent them from doing what they believe to be their duty. And if there are any here present disposed to take up this unfortunate trade, I would assure them that as long as the law punishes, and the magistrates uphold the law, so long will they bring offenders to justice. So long as men say there is no God, or that the religion of the state is a farce and a fallacy, these gentlemen will not be deterred by any clamour.' If this threat were carried out the magistrates on every Bench would have constant employment—especially if they would undertake, as Mr. Bubb appeared to promise, to ascertain whether or not we had the 'flimsiest pretext' to offer in defence of the course we took.

Adams and his wife were committed to take their trials at the

Sessions—in the wife's case it was purely vexatious, as there was no one bound over to prosecute her. Yet Adams, nearly blind from an inflammation of the eyes, and his wife with her child in her arms, were kept several days in attendance at Gloucester—though the same law which prevented the court proceeding in my case, prevented the court from trying the Adamses. In further aggravation of loss, £1 17s. 6d. were demanded for discharge of bail and entering new sureties—nor was time allowed to fetch the bail (after they were demanded) from Cheltenham, the clerk announcing that they would be estreated at once. Upon this I directed Mr. and Mrs. Adams to go into court and say they were prepared to take their trial *then*, and there was no occasion to estreat the property of their friends. Time was then allowed.

Mrs. Adams was never tried. Mr. Adams's trial took place at Gloucester assizes, immediately before my own.

The passage from No. 25 of the *Oracle*, for which Adams was indicted, was written by my friend Mr. Chilton, who was outraged at my imprisonment, and ran as follows:—

What else could be expected of men who deify a real or imaginary individual, a compound of ambition and folly, of mock humility and rampant tyranny; who, though called the ' Prince of Peace,' declared he came to bring a sword in the world? This hellish mission he performed to perfection, for never since his time has blood and misery ceased to flow from his dogmas and mysteries.

As I was very anxious to save Adams from consequences which he incurred through friendship to me, I advised him to let Mr. Thompson defend him. This gentleman began by sympathising with all the disgust invented by the counsel who opened the prosecution, and he ended by expressing Adams's sorrow and contrition for what he had done—a contrition which he did not feel, and would rather have undergone much imprisonment than have had it said that he did. During the whole of the trials arising out of the *Oracle*, Mr. Ralph Thomas, barrister, was the only counsel who defended us in court without sacrificing us. Taking warning by Mr. Thompson's example, I made it a rule to advise all our friends to defend themselves, and where unaccustomed to public speaking, to write a brief defence in their own language, and after some legal friend had revised it, to read it to the court. We do not want lawyers to defend our opinions, those opinions not being their own, but we want them simply to maintain our right to publish what are to us important convictions. Instead of this they commonly agree with the crown that we are criminal for having a conscience, and then, in our name, recant with ' contrition' the opinions which we go into court to maintain.

Adams's sentence was delivered in the following words by Mr. Justice Erskine:—' George Adams, you have been convicted of the offence of publishing a blasphemous libel, and the libel which was proved to have been published by you was one of a most horrid and shocking character. Whatever a man's opinions may be, he can have no right to give vent to them in that language. If there was evidence to prove that you were the author, or that you were engaged as an active disseminator, I should have thought it my duty to have inflicted on you a very serious imprisonment. Although by the law of this country every man has a right to express his sentiments in decent language, he has no business to make use of such shocking language as this. But you have expressed, through your counsel, contrition; and trusting that this is the general feeling of your mind, I shall not think it necessary to pass on you a severe sentence this time. But if you ever offend again, it will then be known that you are determined to persevere, and it will be seen whether the law is not strong enough to prevent it. The sentence of the court is, that you be *imprisoned in the Common Gaol of this county for one calendar month.*'

I was with Adams during the term of his imprisonment, and although his losses and the privations of his family were great, he never uttered a murmuring word. From first to last he behaved well, and Mrs. Adams, as women usually do, behaved better.

It is worthy of remark that when a gentleman deposed that the character of Mr. Adams 'was a pattern of morality,' Mr. Justice Erskine told the jury that 'had Adams committed a robbery such a character might have weight, but in extenuation of religious offence it was of no service.'

CHAPTER II.—THE TRIAL.

The Assizes opened on the 6th of August, 1842, but my case did not come on till the 15th, Mr. Knight Hunt (the author of the 'Fourth Estate') was the gentleman engaged to report my trial. As the judge was informed that I intended to defend myself he resolved to take my case last. This caused the assizes to extend into a second week. Saturday came before the calendar was exhausted, and as there was no knowing whether my trial could be gone through in a day, the fear of trespassing on Sunday led to the court's being ordered to open on Monday, to the annoyance of javelin men kept there unexpectedly, to jury men who had left tills, ploughs, and orange baskets unprotected—and not least to my prosecutors, who saw with some consternation some £200 added to the county expenses, for in Cheltenham bigotry is greatly preferred when it is *cheap*.

If ignorance would look upon its own degradation, let it spend a few hours in an assize court. One trial I witnessed was of two men for an offence which indeed arose out of depravity, but the depravity arose out of bad training and vicious circumstances. The oldest man, between forty and fifty, was sentenced to transportation for life to Norfolk Island, the most ferocious sentence an English judge can pronounce. When the man heard it, he bowed in genuine and awkward humbleness, and said, as he made a rustic bow to the bench, '*Thank'ee, my Lord!*' Such abject humiliation of spirit I had never conceived before. Ignorance never appeared to me so frightful, so slavish, so blind, as on this occasion. Unable to distinguish a sentence passed upon him from a service done him, he had been taught to bow to his pastors and masters, and he bowed alike when cursed as when blessed. The measured contempt with which the words were spoken by the judge which blasted the man's character for ever—the scorn with which he was thrust out of the pale of society, never again to know freedom or reputation, made no impression on his dark and servile soul. That appalling weight of infamy falling on his head and on the heads of his children—for which he might justly have cursed society—only elicited from him a 'Thank'ee, my Lord!' If ignorance would see its own degradation, would feel the incalculable depth of its abjectness, let it sometimes sit for instruction in an assize court.

The preliminary proceedings at the trial I shall render as Mr. Hunt gave them, in the third person—adding what, from various causes, was omitted at the time.

On the morning of the trial the Court-house at Gloucester was very crowded. Many ladies were present from all parts of the county: the wives of clergymen, and some of the nobility, were among them, attracted by curiosity, and by the opportunity which might never occur to them again of hearing, without loss of caste, a little heresy defended in person. The audience continued undiminished till ten o'clock at night.

As the name of George Jacob Holyoake was called, he advanced and entered the dock. Mr. Ogden, the turnkey in charge of prisoners, directed him with the usual air of official impatience to take his place at the bar.

Mr. Holyoake. Do not be in a hurry. First hand me my books.

Mr. Ogden. (Looking indignantly at a large corded box lying outside the dock.) You can't have that box here. You must go to the bar and plead.

Mr. Holyoake. Nonsense. Hand me the box.

It being reluctantly handed up, Mr. Holyoake applied to the judge, Mr. Justice Erskine, for the use of a table.

Mr. Justice Erskine. There is one. (He referred to some boarding behind the bar, and there Mr. Holyoake proceeded to arrange his books and papers—although the situation was not advantageous, it being lower than the bar where the prisoners usually stand. Mr. Holyoake employed twenty minutes in this operation, and when he had done, the dock resembled a young bookseller's stall. Mr. Holyoake then advanced to the bar and bowed to the court.

Mr. Justice Erskine (who had waited with great patience). Are you ready?

Mr. Holyoake replied affirmatively, and the clerk proceeded to read the indictment as follows:—

[GLOUCESTER TO WIT.]—The Jurors for our lady the Queen, upon their oath, present that George Jacob Holyoake, late of the parish of Cheltenham, in the county of Gloucester, labourer,* being a wicked, malicious, and evil-disposed person, and disregarding the laws and religion of the realm, and wickedly and profanely devising and intending to bring Almighty God, the Holy Scriptures, and the Christian religion, into disbelief and contempt among the people of this kingdom, on the twenty-fourth day of May, in the fifth year of the reign of our lady the Queen, with force and arms, at the parish aforesaid, in the county aforesaid, in the presence and hearing of divers liege subjects of our said lady the Queen, maliciously, unlawfully, and wickedly did compose, speak, utter, pronounce, and publish with a loud voice, of and concerning Almighty God, the Holy Scriptures, and the Christian religion, these words following, that is to say, ' I (meaning the said George Jacob Holyoake) do not believe there is such a thing as a God: I (meaning the said George Jacob Holyoake) would have the Deity served as they (meaning the government of this kingdom) serve the subaltern, place him (meaning Almighty God) on half-pay'—to the high displeasure of Almighty God, to the great scandal and reproach of the Christian religion, in open violation of the laws of this kindom, to the evil example of all others in the like case offending, and against the peace of our lady the Queen, her crown and dignity.

Mr. Holyoake pleaded *Not Guilty*, and applied to have the names of the jury called over singly and distinctly.

Mr. Alexander, counsel for the prosecution, said the offence being only a misdemeanour, the defendant had no right to challenge.

Mr. Justice Erskine. Of course not, unless reasons are given in each case.

Clerk. The name of John Lovesey is first.

Mr. Holyoake. I object to Lovesey. He sat on the bench when I was before the magistrates at Cheltenham, and approved the proceedings against me. He is not disinterested in this matter.

Mr. Justice Erskine said that was not sufficient reason for challenging.

---

* It was pure invention that described me as a 'labourer.' It was a term of degradation in the county, and therefore employed—my profession was that of a Mathematical Teacher.

Lovesey declared he 'shuddered at the crime of the prisoner,' and after some further conversation, the judge having observed it was 'as well to go,' Lovesey left the box.

Mr. Holyoake. In the case of Mr. Southwell he was allowed to challenge.

Mr. Justice Erskine. I am not bound by the Recorder of Bristol

The names of the other jurors having been called over, Mr. Holyoake objected to one on the ground of his being a farmer, and from his profession not likely to be acquainted with the nature of the question at issue.*

Mr. Justice Erskine said he could not sit there to listen to such objections. Mr. Holyoake saying he had no objection to urge which his lordship would allow, ' seven farmers, one grocer, one poulterer, one miller, one nondescript shopkeeper, and one maltster, were then impannelled to ascertain whether one George Jacob Holyoake had had a fight with Omnipotence, whether he had done his utmost to bring the Deity into contempt, whether he had fought Omnipotence with force of arms, and had spoken against it or him with a loud voice.'†

The following is the list of the jury:—

Thomas Gardiner, grocer, Cheltenham, Foreman.
James Reeve, farmer, Chedworth.
William Ellis, farmer, Chedworth.
Avery Trotman, farmer, Chedworth.
William Mathews, poulterer, Cheltenham.
Simon Vizard, shopkeeper, Oldland.
Isaac Tombs, farmer, Whitcomb.
William Wilson, maltster, Brimpsfield.
Edwin Brown, farmer, Withington.
Bevan Smith, farmer, Harescomb.
William Smith, miller, Barnwood.
Joseph Shipp, farmer, Yate.

Mr. Holyoake. Can I have a copy of the indictment?

Mr. Justice Erskine. I had one made for you in consequence of your application to the court last week.

Mr. Holyoake. Yes, my lord, but after I had thanked you for your courtesy in so doing, I was asked 8s. 6d. for it by (not being able to call him by his name, Mr. Holyoake said) that sour looking gentleman there, (pointing to the clerk of the court, an individual as dusty and as forbidding as an old penal statute, and who always spoke to Mr. Holyoake like one. The court laughed, the judge frowned, the clerk looked indignant, but before censure could fall, Mr. Holyoake escaped into the next sentence, adding), after the numerous exactions I was subjected to at the

* A poulterer is called upon, under oath, to decide this great theological and philosophical question that has agitated the world for so many hundred centuries....... To make a poulterer a sovereign judge of theology is on a par with making the Archbishop of Canterbury a judge of poultry.—*Weekly Dispatch*, August 18. 1842. [It has been objected to this that very likely his Grace of Canterbury is a very good judge of poultry.]

† 'Publicola's' second letter to Judge Erskine.—*Weekly Dispatch*, Sept. 18, 1842.

sessions, after being brought here by the magistrates and then not tried, I did not think myself justified in paying any more, and the clerk refused it me.

Mr. Justice Erskine. I ordered a copy to be made for you, but did not think it necessary that you should have it on any other than the usual conditions.*

Mr. Holyoake. Can I be allowed to read the indictment against me?

Mr. Justice Erskine. Certainly.

The clerk then handed a copy to Mr. Holyoake, who on observing the counsel for the prosecution rise, left the bar and placed himself where he could face Mr. Alexander, with a view to take notes. The judge very courteously asked if Mr. Holyoake desired note-paper and pens, which he accepted, and :

Mr. Alexander said—Gentlemen of the jury : The defendant at the bar is indicted, not for writing, but for speaking and uttering certain wicked and blasphemous words. This person is not, as in the case previously brought before your attention,† the *vendor*, but he is the *author* of the blasphemy. From the coincidence of words, he is the editor—

Mr. Justice Erskine. You must not proceed in that way. You must not assume—

Mr. Alexander. I am aware, my lord, that I may not assert the identity of the defendant with the work alluded to—I was only going to draw the attention of the gentlemen of the jury to the coincidence of the words. But I will proceed with my case. The defendant, on the 24th of May last, issued placards for a lecture to be delivered in Cheltenham. In these placards he announced, not the diabolical, the dreadful topics which he descanted upon, not anything which would lead the reader to imagine or expect what really took place—but he gave out his subject as a lecture upon Home Colonisation, Emigration, and the Poor Laws. Mark this, gentlemen of the jury. Had he given in his announcements any hint of what was to take place, his end might have been defeated, and no audience attracted to listen to the blasphemous expressions you have heard set out in the indictment. But he did obtain an audience, a numerous audience, and then declared that the people were too poor to have a religion—that he himself had no religion—that he did not believe in such a thing as a God ; and—though it pains me to repeat the horrible blasphemy—that he would place the Deity upon half-pay. I shall call witnesses to prove all this, and then it will be for you to say if he is guilty. It may be urged to you that

* This copy of Indictment occupied *not quite one sheet of paper*, for which *eight shillings and sixpence* were asked !
† That of George Adams.

these things were said in answer to a question, that the *inuendoes* must be made out. *Inuendoes!* I should think it an insult to the understandings of twelve jurymen—of twelve intelligent men —to call witnesses to prove inuendoes: but I shall place the case before you, and leave it in your hands. I am sure I need not speak, I need not dilate upon the consequence of insulting that Deity we are as much bound, as inclined, to reverence. He then called

James Bartram—who said: I am a printer at Cheltenham, employed upon the *Cheltenham Chronicle;* attended the lecture of defendant, just after nine o'clock; there were about one hundred persons present of both sexes; the placard announced 'Home Colonisation, Emigration, Poor Laws Superseded;' heard a man put a question to Mr. Holyoake; he said, 'The lecturer has been speaking of our duty to man, but he has said nothing as regards our duty towards God.' Prisoner replied, 'I am of no religion at all—I do not believe in such a thing as a God. The people of this country are too poor to have any religion. I would serve the Deity as the government does the subaltern—place him on half-pay.' He was the length of the room off; I heard him distinctly; he spoke in a distinct voice.

Cross-examined by Mr. Holyoake. You say I said the people were too poor to have any religion; will you state the reasons I gave?

Witness. I can give the substance, if not the words; you said, 'The great expense of religion to the country.'

Mr. Holyoake. I will thank you to state the other reasons?

Witness. I don't recollect any other reason.

Mr. Holyoake. Now, you have sworn the words are blasphemous—

Mr. Justice Erskine. No, he has not.

Mr. Holyoake. Will you state if the words are blasphemous?

Mr. Justice Erskine said such a question could only be put through him. He then put the question—do you consider the words blasphemous?

Witness. I do.

Mr. Holyoake. Why do you think them blasphemous?

Witness. Because they revile the majesty of heaven, and are calculated to subvert peace, law, and order; and are punishable by human law, because they attack human authority.

Mr. Holyoake. Who has instructed you to define blasphemy thus?

Witness. I have not been instructed, it is my own opinion.

Mr. Holyoake. At Cheltenham, during my examination before the magistrates, you did not appear to have these notions. Will you swear you have not concocted that answer for this occasion?

Witness. I did not expect such a question would be put; I did not expect to be catechised.

Mr. Holyoake. Who advised you to attend as a witness?

Witness. The magistrates sent for me.

Mr. Holyoake. Did you not know before the day of my commitment something of this matter?

Witness. There was some 'chaff' in the office about it; that's all I heard of it; a policeman was sent from the magistrates for me to give the names of witnesses who were to appear. Don't know why the policeman came to me; don't know his name; no clergyman has spoken to me, that I recollect, upon the subject of this prosecution; not sure of it; several persons have spoken to me, cannot say they were clergymen; I do not know the parties who got up the prosecution, or sent the policeman to me; the report was furnished to the paper I work on by another person; I saw the reporter's notes, but not the editor's observations till the galleys were pulled.

Mr. Justice Erskine. What do you mean by galleys pulled?

Witness. Brass slides, my lord.

Mr. Justice Erskine. You mean, I suppose, till all the types were up?

Witness. Yes, my lord.

Cross-examination resumed. Do not know of my own knowledge who made the report; have been ten years in employment at *Chronicle* office; know it was said in that paper that three witnesses from that office could prove what had occurred at the lecture; the name of reporter of our paper is Edward Wills; I heard your lecture, you said nothing against morality.

Mr. Holyoake. Will you state your opinion of morality?

Mr. Justice Erskine. The question is irrelevant.

Mr. Holyoake. Did you think I spoke my honest convictions?

Witness. I thought you spoke what you meant; you spoke straightforwardly.

The judge here interposed, to stop Mr. Holyoake from asking as to witness's opinions.

Cross-examination resumed—Witness. I should not have lost my situation if I had not come forward in this case; in my opinion you spoke wickedly, as stated in indictment; I did not notice that you spoke contemptuously when using the word *thing*, but you used the word; there were other words between those used in indictment; they did not, as in that document, follow one another; I do not remember the words; you spoke of the enormous sums of money spent upon religion, and the poverty of the people, and afterwards, and in connection with that, said you would place Deity as government did the subalterns—on half-pay; I have been a preacher.

Re-examined by Mr. Alexander. I have been uninterruptedly ten years in the same employment; do not give evidence from fear or reward; but from a sense of duty.

Mr. Alexander. That is the case for the prosecution, my lord.

Mr. Justice Erskine. Now is the time for your defence.

Mr. Holyoake. I am not a little surprised to hear that the case for the prosecution is closed. I have heard nothing, not one word, to prove the charge in the indictment. There has been adduced no evidence to show that I have uttered words *maliciously* and *wickedly* blasphemous. I submit to your lordship that there is not sufficient evidence before the Court.

Mr. Justice Erskine. That is for the jury to decide.

Mr. Holyoake. I thought, my lord, as the evidence is so manifestly insufficient to prove *malice*, you would have felt bound to direct my acquittal.

Mr. Justice Erskine. It is for the jury to say whether they are satisfied.

Mr. Holyoake. Then, Gentlemen of the Jury, it now becomes my duty to address you on the nature of the charge preferred against me, and of the evidence by which it is attempted to be supported. When I stood in this court a week ago, and saw the grand jury with Mr. Grantley Berkeley at their head as foreman—when I heard his lordship, surrounded by learned counsel, deliver his charge in the midst of persons distinguished for learning, for eloquence, for experience, and for literary attainments—I then thought, as I now do, that this court could find nobler means than the employment of brute force to counteract anything I could attempt—which I never have done—to bring the truly sacred into contempt. I thought I never should be called upon to stand in this dock, with all its polluting and disgusting associations, to answer for mere matters of speculative opinion. I did think that such persons possessed a sense of the powers of the human mind that would have prevented the interposition of penal judges upon such subjects.

But to Mr. Grantley Berkeley, as foreman of the grand jury who found a true bill against me, I beg to draw your attention. Mr. Grantley Berkeley, as you are aware, is brother to the member, Mr. C. Berkeley, who attempted to vindicate the conduct of the Cheltenham magistrates from the allegations against them by Sir James Graham in the House of Commons. In the recent case of Mr. Mason, who was taken from a meeting, as I was at Cheltenham, by a policeman, illegally, without a warrant, the doctrine was laid down by a cabinet minister, in the House of Commons, that if the person so arrested was subsequently found guilty by a jury, the illegal apprehension was justified. See how this applies to my case. I was taken from a public meeting a

week after the objectionable words were spoken; was taken by a policeman at near midnight; without a warrant. This was justly deemed illegal. I sat in the gallery of the House of Commons when the Hon. Member for Bath brought forward my case, and when Sir James Graham, in reference to the correspondence which had taken place with the magistrates, had the frankness to say, 'there had been serious irregularities and unnecessary harshness used in the case of Holyoake.' In this country four thousand applications are annually made to the Secretary of State for the Home Department, and out of that four thousand my case is spoken of as one in which serious irregularities had occurred, and unnecessary harshness been employed. And that amid the numerous affairs of this great empire it should have received this distinct notice is presumptive evidence that it contained much that should be corrected. On Thursday, July 21, the Hon. Mr. C. Berkeley, addressing the Speaker of the House of Commons, said, 'I wish to ask the Right Hon. Baronet the Secretary for the Home Department a question, but in order to make it intelligible to the House, it will be necessary for me to refer to what took place on Tuesday last. It appears that upon that day the Hon. Member for Bath stated, " that as a person named Holyoake had been committed to prison, at Cheltenham, in an improper manner, he wished to know whether the Right Hon. the Secretary for the Home Department had any objection to produce the correspondence which had taken place upon that subject"—to which the Right Hon. Baronet replied that, " he felt called on in the discharge of his duty to inquire into the circumstances of the commitment in question—he found that serious irregularities had been committed, and he expressed his opinion to that effect—but as legal proceedings were likely to result out of what had occurred, he did not think it would be judicious in the Hon. and learned Gentleman to press for the production of the correspondence."...
.... The Right Hon. Baronet knows, or at least ought to know, that no such imputation could with propriety be cast upon the magistrates, for by the 3rd section of the 2nd and 3rd of Victoria, commonly called the County Constabulary Act, no magistrate or magistrates, in petty sessions assembled, can interfere with or control the chief constable, or any sub-constable, in the discharge of their duties, as the rules and regulations for these all emanate from the office of the Right Hon. Baronet. It therefore was exceedingly unfair that these imputations should go forth, and I have therefore now to ask, on behalf of the magistrates, whether the Right Hon. Baronet objects to the correspondence being printed and circulated with the votes of the house, and in case he should object I shall offer it for the perusal of the Hon. Member

for Bath.' Sir James Graham, in reply, said, 'I had no intention whatever to cast any imputation on the gentlemen, who that day formed the Petty Sessions. My observation more properly applied to the capture of Holyoake, and the unnecessary harshness used in his conveyance from the magistrates' office. At the same time I shall object to the printing of the correspondence with the votes, as no good result would come from it. Of course the hon. member is at liberty to offer it to the Hon. Member for Bath if he chooses—but I repeat, that as legal proceedings were pending, I think such course not advisable.'

This is a most flagrant attempt at justification. The Act the hon. member quoted related to Petty Session magistrates, before whom he knew my case had never come, and of whom, therefore, no complaint could have been made. But Mr. Berkeley had a friendly purpose to serve. The magistrates and their friends have the strongest motives for finding a true bill against me—and they have motives equally powerful for desiring that your verdict should be 'guilty,' inasmuch as that verdict will justify all these 'irregularities'—all the 'unnecessary harshness'—will remove from their shoulders all the responsibility which they incurred by the course they have pursued towards me. Bear in mind, gentlemen of the jury, if the rights are to be enjoyed about which we so much glorify ourselves, cases of this kind must not be allowed to pass unnoticed. 'Serious irregularities' demand serious notice. Arbitrary infraction of the liberty of the subject must not receive the sanction of a jury. Recollect that the same course may be pursued towards any one of you, and that if it receives your sanction it will be made a precedent of law—and pernicious may be its influence.

But I would draw your attention to a printed report of remarks, made by his lordship, in his charge to the grand jury upon my case. I do not for a moment believe that his lordship had other than fair intentions, but, unfortunately, his remarks will have a contrary effect on those who have to judge my case. I have in my hand the *Cheltenham Chronicle*, of Wednesday last, August 10th, from which I will read. 'These offences,' he said, referring to the cases of blasphemy, 'lay at the root of all the crime which prevailed, and a consideration of the causes out of which they sprung pointed to the only efficient remedy for their removal. In the case of Holyoake, his lordship observed that a work called the *Oracle of Reason* had been printed and circulated containing language which he did not think it right to repeat; language in which the writer traced all the evil which existed in the world, not to the real cause—the evil passions of the human heart—but to the existence of Christianity itself. This was followed by the most opprobrious language'—

Mr. Justice Erskine (interrupting). I never said anything of the kind -that printed report is entirely incorrect.

Mr. Holyoake. I will read some notes of your lordship's charge, taken at the time of its delivery by a reporter. But whether the report in the *Chronicle* is correct or incorrect, it has had its influence in leading the public, and probably this jury, to a prejudgment of my case.

'There are other charges which seem at once to lead the mind to the consideration of the root of all the evil which forms the subject of our present consideration. I allude to two charges of blasphemy. In one the accused is said to have sold and published a paper called the *Oracle of Reason* containing language which I shall not think it right to read, in which the writer traces the evils at present existing, not to the evil passions of man, but to the existence of Christianity, and follows it up with the most opprobrious language to the Saviour and his system, charging him with being the occasion of all the crime and misery which prevail. The second charge is against a man who gave a lecture, in the course of which he discussed the proper way of teaching man his duty to his neighbour. A person *suggested* that he had said nothing about teaching man his duty to his God. That led to a statement which shows the folly of the person; and he followed it up by making use of such language that, if you believe it was intended to have destroyed the reverence for God, he has subjected himself to punishment. There is another thing—he does not appear to have intended to discuss this; but if you are convinced that, by what he has said, he intended to bring religion into contempt, he is guilty of blasphemy. If such addresses had been directed to the educated classes, it might have been thought they would remedy themselves; but when they are delivered among persons not educated, the greatest danger might be expected. It is not by the punishment of those who attempt to mislead the ignorant that we can hope to cure the evil. If we feel that it is from the ignorance of those persons to whom the addresses are delivered that the danger is to be apprehended, it becomes our imperative duty to teach those persons. Some persons have said, "Instruct the poor in reading and writing, but leave them to learn religion at home." But what would you say to a man who would manure his land, and leave it to find seed for itself? It would produce nothing but weeds. I know there is great difficulty in arranging any national schools; but, as we are all individually sufferers, I hope we shall join in extending a national religious education, so that all may learn to do right, not from a fear of punishment, but from a far nobler motive—the knowledge that offences against the laws are contrary to the precepts of the word of God, and hostile to the best interests of society.'

I fear his lordship may not give me credit for sincerity; but I do assure you, gentlemen of the jury, no one heard *some* of those sentiments with more pleasure than I did. I did not expect so much liberality. If such advice had been followed, I should not now be standing here to defend points of a speculative nature. Such errors should be corrected by argument, in the arena of public opinion. Where I uttered these words, they should have been refuted. The witness against me says he is a preacher; had he no word in answer? could he say no word for his God? No; he, and those who employ and abet him, shrink from the attempt, and seek to punish in this dock opinions they cannot refute. Is this a course becoming those who say they have *truth* on their side?

His lordship said 'emissaries are going about.' I am no emissary, and the term as applied to me is unjust. I might, even by the admission of Mr. Bubb, 'undermine' men's religion, go about secretly disseminating my opinions, without danger of standing here. But I spoke openly; and you who usually have to punish *dishonesty*, are now called upon to punish its non-committal, for a little lying would have saved me from this charge. I have infringed no law, injured no man's reputation, taken no man's property, attacked no man's person, broken no promise, violated no oath, encouraged no evil, taught no immorality—set only an example of free speaking. I was asked a question, and answered it openly. I am not even charged with declaring dogmatically, 'There is no God.' I only expressed an opinion. I should hold myself degraded could I descend to inquire, before uttering my convictions, if they met the approval of every anonymous man in the audience. I never forget that other men's opinions may be correct—that others may be right as well as myself. I have put forth my own opinions openly, from a conviction of their truth; and the sentiments I cannot defend I should scorn like my prosecutors to invoke an attorney-general to protect. I seek a public place, where any man may refute me if he can, and convict me as wilful or ignorant. I should think myself degraded if I published secretly. What can we think of the morality of a law which requires secret inquiry, which prohibits the *free* publication of opinion?

Mr. Justice Erskine. You must have heard me state the law, that if it be done seriously and decently all men are at liberty to state opinions.

Mr. Holyoake. Whatever the law says, if an informer can carry the words to persons interested in their suppression—if policemen can be sent to apprehend, without warrants, the man who publicly expresses his opinions—if he can be handcuffed like a felon, and thrust into a gaol—if indictments can be brought against him, and he be put to ruinous expenses and harassing anxieties, however honest the expression of opinion may be—then, I say, this 'liberty-law' is a mockery. But by the word 'decent' is meant 'what those in authority think proper.' There should be no censorship of opinions; but I am told that because I spoke to ignorant people, I am criminal. To educated persons, then, I might have said what I did with impunity—

Mr. Justice Erskine. I only, after speaking of education, said that an honest man, speaking his opinions decently, was entitled to do so.

Mr. Holyoake. There is no evidence to show that my audience were unable to distinguish decency and propriety. But it must be already clear enough to you, gentlemen of the jury, who have been employed during the past week determining violations of the law, that I am placed here for having been more honest than the law happens to allow. I am unaccustomed to address a jury, and I hope to avoid the charge of presumption or dogmatism. I have no wish to offend the prejudices of any man in this court, and have no interest in so doing, when his lordship is armed with the power of the law to punish it. But, while I profess respect for your opinions, I must entertain some for my own. There are those here who think religion proper, and that it alone can lead to general happiness—I do not, and I have had the sam means of judging. You say your feelings are insulted—your opinions outraged; but what of mine? Mine, however honest, are rendered liable to punishment. I ask not equality of privileges in this respect; I seek not the power of punishing those who differ from me —nay, I should disdain its use. Christianity claims what she does not allow, although she says 'All men are brothers.'

It is from no disrespect to the bar that I did not give my case into the hands of counsel, but because they are unable to enter into my motives. There is a magic circle out of which they will not step; they will argue only what is orthodox; and you would have had no opportunity from them of learning my true motives, or seeing the real bearings of this case.*

The author of the paragraph which led to this day's proceedings applied to me the epithets of 'wretch,' 'miscreant,' 'monster'— represented me as one who discoursed 'devilism.' The *Gloucester Chronicle* laboured to prove that I was a *malicious* blasphemer.

* From what subsequently appeared in the *Cheltenham Free Press*, I learned that some of the bar took offence at these remarks; and one revenged himself by describing me, in the *Morning Chronicle*, as 'a wretched-looking creature, scarcely emerging from boyhood, whose wiry and dishevelled hair, "lip unconscious of the razor's edge," and dingy looks, gave him the appearance of a low German student, is evidently, from his pronunciation and language, a most ignorant and illiterate character, and no doubt courted the present prosecution for the sake of notoriety.'

The *Cheltenham Examiner*—the editor of which, I understand, is Mr. Jelinger Symons—draws a parallel between me and the reputed regicide, who has recently shot at the Queen. These are the words:—' Akin to the offence for which Holyoake has been committed is the crime for which Francis, also a mere stripling, is likely to forfeit his personal liberty, if not his life. The crimes of blasphemy and treason have many points of great similarity, and frequently result from the same causes; and it would not be an uninstructive task to trace out the progress of those causes which lead the minds of the unguarded to the extreme points when they become dangerous to society. Holyoake, the bold assertor of the non-existence of a God, did not become an infidel at once; and Francis, the would-be regicide, did not level his pistol at our beloved sovereign without his mind having been acted and prepared by previous circumstances...... In both cases a morbid imagination, an affectation of superiority, a contempt for and a dissatisfaction with existing institutions, and a craving after notoriety, are the primary incentives to action.' This ungenerous and offensive parallel was drawn out through a long leading article. The effect, if not the object, of all this is to prejudge my case, to awaken all the bitter prejudices which lurk around religion, and to secure my condemnation before my trial.

Another paper,* in which justice was done me in some respects, called me a 'bigot.' I am not a bigot. I do not assume that I alone am right; nor did I speak of Deity, declaring dogmatically his non-existence. I spoke only of my own disbelief in such an existence. Of all *isms* I think dogmatism the worst. I do not judge other men by the agreement of their opinions with my own. I believe you consider Christianity a benefit. I regret that I feel it is not so, and I claim the privilege of saying what is true to me. I have ever been ready to acquire correct notions. I have publicly called upon parties whose duty it was to teach me—and who were well paid for teaching—to assist me in sifting out the truth. But they have chosen the strong arm of the law rather than strong argument. Jean Jacques Rousseau says in his 'Confessions,' 'Enthusiasm for sublime virtue is of little use in society. In aiming too high we are subject to fall; the continuity of little duties, well fulfilled, demands no less strength than heroic actions, and we find our account in it much better, both in respect to reputation and happiness. The constant esteem of mankind is infinitely better than sometimes their admiration.' As the world goes there is much good sense in this, and I have read it to show how fully I accord with these sentiments. I am not aiming at sublime virtue, but rather at the continuity of little duties well fulfilled. It is enough for me if I can be true and useful.

* The *National Association Gazette*.

I was greatly surprised to find the learned gentleman engaged as prosecuting counsel had so little to say in reference to the case entrusted to his charge, but I presume it must be attributed to the fact that little could be said upon the subject. All his ingenuity, all his legal skill could not discover an argument at all tenable against me. I certainly expected to hear him attempt to prove to you that these prosecutions were either useful or necessary, but he could only tell you that my sentiments were very horrible, without adducing proof that his assertions were true. He dealt liberally in inuendoes, particularly in reference to the placards exhibited previous to the lecture, and the motive for issuing them. But you have been able to glean from his own witness the truth of the matter. I had completed my discourse, which was of a secular character, and was preparing to return home, when one Maitland questioned me on the subject of my opinions. I did not get up a meeting under one pretence to use it for another. I employed no scheme to allure an audience to listen to what I did not openly avow, although it has been unfairly insinuated that I did so.

When I was first apprehended my papers were taken from me. They would not even leave me the papers necessary for my defence, and I do not know what use was made of them, or that this day the information thus unfairly obtained may not be employed against me. I will read the memorial on this subject, which I forwarded to the Secretary of State.

'*Memorial of the undersigned George Jacob Holyoake, prisoner in Gloucester County Gaol, on the charge of Blasphemy, to Sir James Graham, Her Majesty's Secretary of State,*

'SHEWETH,—That your memorialist was committed to this gaol from Cheltenham, on the vague charge of blasphemy, on June 3rd.

'That in consequence of representations made to him by the police authorities in Cheltenham, your memorialist brought with him to the gaol some private papers, hastily selected, for his defence—and that, on arriving here, the said papers were seized, and the visiting magistrate refused to allow your memorialist the use of them, or to give them up to his friends to be used for his advantage.

'That, as these papers were brought in confidence that your memorialist would have been allowed to consult his own thoughts in his own defence—and as they are no man's property but his own—and, also, as without them your memorialist will not have a fair chance of defence,—he trusts you will order them to be restored to him without delay.

'The offence with which your memorialist stands charged occurred as he was journeying homeward, in a town where he was a comparative stranger. Consequently, and owing to great bigotry on religious subjects, your memorialist has been unable to obtain bail, and has suffered fourteen days' imprisonment, which time he has spent in fruitless applications to the authorities here for proper books and papers to prepare his defence. Out of a list of thirty-one books submitted for that purpose only thirteen are allowed.

'That, as the trial of your memorialist is to take place at the next sessions of this county, to be holden on the 28th inst., and he is without the means of defence or hope of justice, and has a wife and two children dependent on him for support, he is placed in circumstances of peculiar anxiety.

'Hence your memorialist earnestly hopes that you will direct that his papers, seized as before mentioned, be immediately restored to him, and also that he be allowed free access to such works and papers as he may deem necessary for his defence, and that without further delay.

'(Signed)   GEORGE JACOB HOLYOAKE.

'County Gaol, Gloucester, June 14, 1842.'

The papers were *afterwards* returned ; but, had it not been for friends in the House of Commons, and in various parts of the country, I should have been deprived of the materials for my defence. Public opinion did for me that which Christian charity refused.*

Strong prejudices exist against me as being a Socialist. Your local newspapers have denounced me on this ground. To show that I deserve no condemnation on this account I shall draw your attention to the nature of Socialism. I have here a little book, stated to be published by the 'Society for Promoting Christian Knowledge.' If it had been stated to be a 'society' for disseminating ' malicious knowledge' the title-page would have been correct—for a more gross series of misrepresentations were never strung together. If what it says of Socialism were true, then I might be abused ; but Socialism as I have learned or explained it, would never lead to the injury of peace or the disturbance of public order. The first paragraph of Godwin's ' Political Justice' is an epitome of Socialism as developed in this country hitherto : it is 'an investigation concerning that form of political society, that system of intercourse and reciprocal action extending beyond the bounds of a single family, which shall be found most conducive to the *general* benefit—how may the peculiar and independent operation of each individual in the social state most effectually be preserved—how may the security each man ought to possess as to his life, and the employments of his faculties according to the dictates of his own understanding, be most certainly defended from invasion—how may the individuals of the human species be made to contribute most substantially to general improvement and happiness.' But I shall not content myself with one authority ; and to avoid the charge of presumption, I have gathered much of my defence from other men's writings, and shall make them speak for me.

Socialists have been declared to have dangerous metaphysical

* At the Gloucester Trinity Sessions, Mr. R. B. Cooper stated, in contradiction of the prayer of this memorial, that ' *as soon as I mentioned* that my papers were necessary for my defence they were returned to me.' Mr. S. Jones said he ' took my papers home, and *every one* I wanted for my trial on the morrow I had given to me.' Both these statements were untrue, and I stated so at the time in the *Cheltenham Free Press*, and my assertion was never impugned.

notions. The whole question has been expressed by the poet-philosopher Goethe in four lines, translated by Ebenezer Elliott, thus:—

> How like a stithy is this land!
> And we lie on it, like good metal
> Long hammer'd by a senseless hand;
> But will such thumping make a kettle?

Meaning that senseless hammering and senseless legislation could neither make the dull iron into a kettle, nor a vicious people into an enlightened nation. Socialism says, all men have in them the true metal—the elements of goodness, which all governments are responsible for moulding. Socialism proposes to substitute other means than punishments for the prevention of crime, and that you may not think these chimeras of my own, I will read you the opinion of a Lord Cardinal to a certain High Chancellor of England, Sir Thomas More, who, in his 'Utopia,' says, 'When I was in England, the king depended much on his councils..... One day when I was dining with him there happened to be at table one of the English lawyers, who took occasion to run out in high commendation of the severe execution of justice upon thieves, "who," as he said, "were then hanged so fast that there were sometimes twenty on one gibbet!" and upon that he said, "he could not wonder enough how it came to pass, that since so few escaped there were so many thieves left, who were still robbing in all places." Upon this, I (who took the boldness to speak freely before the cardinal) said, "there was no reason to wonder at the matter, since this way of punishing thieves was *neither just in itself nor good for the public*; for as the severity was too great, so the remedy was not effectual; simple theft not being so great a crime, that it ought to cost a man his life: no punishment, how severe soever, being able to restrain those from robbing who can find no other way of livelihood. In this (said I) not only you in England but a great part of the world, imitate some ill masters, that are readier to chastise their scholars than teach them. There are dreadful punishments enacted against thieves, *but it were much better to make such good provisions by which every man might be put in a method how to live, and so be preserved from the fatal necessity of stealing, and of dying for it.*" Socialism would try to obtain a remedy for the evils which judges go round year by year lamenting; Socialism would suggest a means of affording employment, and thus mitigate the crime which judges and juries are called to punish.

Such objects may be declared chimerical, but surely it is not criminal to hope that they can be carried out, and to feel that they ought. I could read many other passages to show that under no circumstance Socialism merits that character which has been ascribed to it. But I do not deem it necessary, as I think I have said enough to prove that. Nor do I want to instil my sentiments, but merely to disabuse your minds of a prejudice which has been disseminated to my disadvantage.

My assuming the right of free expression inculcated by Mr. Owen, and when asked a question, refusing to equivocate, are opposed, it would appear, to the laws of this country. But this I have learned from Socialism, that there can be no public or private virtue, unless the foundation of action is the practice of truth. Passing through Cheltenham to pay a visit to a friend, I delivered a lecture. After which the words were uttered which are here indicted. When I had read the *Cheltenham Chronicle*, in the city of Bristol, I returned to Cheltenham. If I had been conscious of guilt, should I have returned? On the night of my apprehension marks of kindness were shown me by the people. If I had acted disgracefully, would the people of Cheltenham have met a stranger and showed him marks of esteem and friendship? I went to the station-house and remained there all night. When taken before the magistrates, Mr. Capper told me I was not fit to be reasoned with, because I did not believe in a God, and that it was from a love of notoriety that I acted: but from the love of mere notoriety I have never uttered any sentiments, for I hold such conduct in contempt. After I was taken from the magistrates' office, I was treated with contumely at the police-station. Surgeon Pinching, finding me completely in his power, said he was sorry the days were gone by when I could hold up my head, and wished the inquisition could be put in force against such persons as myself. I was thrust into a filthy cell, and my hands were bolted together and the skin pinched off. I was brought to Gloucester on a sultry day, and should have been made to walk had not some friends interfered and obtained permission for me to ride, on paying my own fare and that of two policemen. There was no indication from my manner that I wished to make my escape, and the company of two policemen was sufficient to prevent it. It was thought if I was chained like a felon and dragged through two towns, it would wound my feelings. If these are the ways in which the truths of Christianity are to be taught, I leave you to judge of them. Two of your magistrates conversed with me, and shouted with much rudeness that I was a fool for holding my opinions. I never could have said this to any man, and yet such treatment I received from magistrates old enough to be my grandfathers.

Here Mr. Bransby Cooper, who sat upon the left of the Judge, was so moved by this remark, that he rose and ejaculated something in Court; but the Judge peremptorily commanded him to sit down.

Mr. Holyoake then read the memorial of the public meeting of the inhabitants of Cheltenham, before quoted, referring to the conduct, at the examination, of Joseph Overbury, Robert Capper, and the Rev. T. B. Newell, D.D., magistrates.

Mr. Justice Erskine. You ought not to read any statement not authenticated by evidence, which reflects on any person.

Defendant. This is a petition of a public meeting.

Mr. Justice Erskine. It is not evidence.

Defendant continued. I have never been anxious under any circumstances to obtrude my opinions on the public. I confined myself strictly to the subject on which I lectured, and should not have introduced my sentiments on religion, should not have spoken another word after my lecture, if I had not been publicly questioned. I have held various situations, and in all secular ones I have strictly kept religious opinions out of view. It is known that I have taught that and that only which I have been employed to teach. In proof of this I may cite testimonials given me upon the occasion of my applying for the situation of collector at the Birmingham Botanic Gardens. They are from magistrates and gentlemen of Birmingham, and the post was one requiring a person of trust, as considerable funds would have to pass through his hands in a year.

Mr. Holyoake here quoted from numerous testimonials. One of them, from a magistrate, F. Lloyd, Esq., stated that 'Mr. Holyoake obtained the first prize at the Mechanics' Institute, some years ago, for proficiency in mathematics, a proficiency attained, too, under most discouraging circumstances.' Another of the testimonials was from the Rev. S. Bache, one of the ministers of the New Meeting House congregation. Having read these documents, Mr. Holyoake resumed.

During one of those commercial panics, which a few years ago passed over this country like a pestilence, my parents were suddenly reduced from a state of comparative affluence to one of privation. At one of these seasons my little sister became ill. While she was so the Rev. Mr. Moseley, M.A., Rector of St. Martin's, Birmingham, sent an order to us for his Easter due of fourpence. On previous occasions this demand had been cheerfully and promptly paid; but now, small as the sum was, it was sufficient materially to diminish the few comforts our house of illness unfortunately afforded; and it was therefore discussed whether the demand of the clergyman should be paid, or whether it should be expended in the purchase of some little comforts for my sick sister. Humanity decided; and we all agreed that it should be devoted to this latter purpose. It was; but, I think, the very next week, a summons came for the Easter due, and two shillings and sixpence were added, because of the non-payment of the *fourpence*. The payment of this could now no longer be evaded, for in a few days a warrant of *distraint* would have rudely torn the bed from under her, as had been the case with a near neighbour. Dreading this, and trembling at the apprehension, we gathered together all the money we had, and which was being saved to purchase a little wine to moisten the parched lips of my dying sister, for at this time her end seemed approaching. My mother, with a heavy heart, left home to go to the Public Office. The aisles there were cold and cheerless like the outside this court, and there, all broken in health and spirits, worn out with watching, and distracted by that anxiety for her child a parent, under such circumstances, only could feel, she was kept from five to six hours waiting to pay the two shillings and tenpence. When she returned all was over—my sister was dead. Gentlemen, will you wonder if, after this, I doubted a little the utility of church establishments?* and if, after the circumstances I have related, I did not think so highly of church 'as by law established' as before, can you be surprised? Can you punish me for it? [At this point many ladies wept, and the Court manifested considerable attention.] I have been told to look around the world for evidences of the truth of the Christian religion; to look upon the world and draw different conclusions. It is well for those who enjoy the smiles of fortune to say so. For them all shines brightly—for them all is fair. But I can see cause of complaint, and I am not alone in the feeling. Mr. Capel Lofft had said, ' the sours of life less offend my taste than its sweets delight it.' On this Kirke White wrote:—

> Go to the raging sea, and say ' Be still !'
> Bid the wild lawless winds obey thy will;
> Preach to the storm, and reason with despair—
> But tell not misery's son *that life is fair*.
>
> Thou, who in plenty's lavish lap hast roll'd,
> And every year with new delight hast told—
> Thou, who, recumbent on the lacquer'd barge,
> Hast dropt down joy's gay stream of pleasant marge,
> *Thou* may'st extol life's calm, untroubled sea—
> The storms of misery ne'er burst on *thee*.
> Go to the mat where squalid want reclines ;
> Go to the shade obscure where merit pines;
> Abide with him whom Penury's charms control,
> And bind the rising yearnings of his soul—
> Survey his sleepless couch, and, standing there,
> Tell the poor pallid wretch *that life is fair*!

---

* I have since learned that Mr. W. J. Fox read this passage in a Sunday morning lecture on the events of the month, delivered at South place in the September following my trial; and I take this opportunity of acknowledging that Mr. Fox was the only occupant of a pulpit from whom I received a friendly line during my entire imprisonment.

> Lo! o'er his manly form, decay'd and wan,
> The shades of death with gradual steps steal on;
> And the pale mother, pining to decay,
> Weeps, for her boy, her wretched life away.
>
> Go, child of fortune! to his early grave,
> Where o'er his head obscure the rank weeds wave;
> Behold the heart-wrung parent lay her head
> On the cold turf, and ask to share his bed.
> Go, child of fortune, take thy lesson there,
> And tell us then that life is *wondrous fair*.

As I grew up I attended missionary meetings, and my few pence were given to that cause. When told of heathen kings who knew not God, and caged their miserable victims, I shuddered at their barbarity and prayed for their conversion. O waste of money and prayers that should have been employed on Christian men. O infantile fatuity! Do I not reap the whirlwind for my pains? I learned the accents of piety from my mother's lips. She was and still is a religious woman. Whatever may be the dissent I entertain, I have never spoken of her opinions in the language of contempt. I have always left her (as she to her honour has left me), to enjoy her own opinions. In early youth I was religious. I question whether there is any here who have spent more time than I did as a Sunday school teacher. I have given hours, which I ought to have employed in improving myself, in improving others. It is not without giving to Christianity time and attention—without knowing what it was—that I have given it up. Some lines I contributed to a religious publication at that time, will show the tone of thought which inquiry has subsequently changed:—

THE REIGN OF TIME.

> The proudest earthly buildings show,
>   Time can all things devour;
> E'en youth and beauty's ardent glow,
> And manhood's intellectual brow,
>   Betray the spoiler's power:
> How soon we sink beneath his sway—
> He glances, and our heads turn gray.
>
> Though, over all this earthly ball,
>   Time's standard is unfurled,
> And ruins loud to ruins call
>   Throughout this time-worn world—
> Yet from this wreck of earthly things,
> See how the soul exulting springs.
>
> And after the archangel's wand
>   Has wav'd o'er earth and sea,
> And Time has stopped at his command,
> The soul will flourish and expand
>   Through all eternity.
> Religion—lovely, fair, and free—
> Holds forth this immortality.

> By all the glories of the sky,
>   To mortals yet unknown—
> And by the worm that ne'er shall die,
>   The fires that always burn—
> By all that's awful or sublime,
> Ye sons of men improve your time.*

It was stated by one of the magistrates that my being of no religion was no crime. I may conclude from what I heard this morning that I am not to be punished for not being religious. It was argued in the *Cheltenham Chronicle* that my expressing my opinions was no crime, and I was at some loss to know what my crime was. The charge stated I was guilty of *blasphemy*. In the depositions made against me, it is stated that I was brought before the Cheltenham magistrates on a charge of FELONY. I believe now what I have to answer is the accusation of uttering certain words offensive to the *Cheltenham Chronicle*.

This paper stated that 'three persons were ready to give evidence on the matter.' And yet the witness says he knew nothing of it till the policeman came for him. He says they were 'chaffing' about my remarks in the office—that is, joking upon them. It does not say much for his seriousness—reporting these 'horrid sentiments' at night, and the next morning '*chaffing*' about them. If it was an aggravation of my crime to have chosen an innocent subject, what would the learned counsel have said if I had chosen a guilty one? It has been sworn by the witnesses that I said I did not believe there was such a *thing* as a God, and an attempt has been made to make you believe that I used the term 'thing' contemptuously, but the witness admits that I did not use it in a contemptuous sense. The same word occurs in some lines by Thomas Moore:—

> Man, in the sunshine of the world's new spring,
> Shall walk transparent like some holy *thing*.

I must have used the word 'thing' in some such sense as it is used in these lines.

It is laid down by the Common Law, that a person denying the existence of a God is a blasphemer. It has not been shown that I did this. I merely stated my disbelief—and disbelief is not included by the law. There is a great difference between denial and disbelief. If I had said distinctly 'there is no God,' it would have been stating that I was quite sure of it. I could not have said that, because I am not sure of it. I saw reasons for disbelief, but did not assert denial. Disbelief is all I profess. Those dogmatise who affirm, rather than those who deny a proposition. Mr. Southwell put this point in its proper light:—

* 'Baptist Tract Magazine,' Vol. ii., p. 341.

'If God had never been affirmed, he could not have been denied. It is a rule of logic, and a very sensible rule, that the *onus probandi*, that is the burthen or weight of proving, rests on those who affirm a proposition. Priests have affirmed the existence of a God, but who will maintain that they have complied with the rule of logic?'*

We can only, I think, arrive at a conviction of the existence of a God by the following modes:—

1. By the medium of *innate ideas*, which we are said by some divines to possess, and which intuitively lead us to entertain the idea of a God.

2. By the *senses*, the sole media by which all *knowledge* is acquired.

3. By *conjecture*.—This is employed by those who suppose there must be a God from their inability otherwise to account for the existence of the universe, and are not willing to allow it to be inexplicable.

4. By *analogy*.—Comparison is the basis of this argument. Analogy is the foundation of natural theology.

5. By *revelation*.—In this country the Bible is said to contain the revelation of a God.

Of these it may be remarked:—

1. *Innate ideas.*—With regard to these, very conclusive reasons have been advanced by eminent philosophers for disbelieving that we have any. And human experience confirms this conclusion. Some nations, as the people of the Arru Islands, have no idea of a God. So this source of knowledge concerning one is, to say the least, dubious.

2. *Senses.*—'No man hath seen God at any time,' is a sufficient reply to this—for the same may be affirmed of every other sense, which is here affirmed of sight.

3. *Conjecture.*—This defies us. We only prove our own inability and multiply difficulties. For when we suppose a God, we cannot suppose how he came, nor how he created something out of nothing, which is held by the learned to be plainly *impossible*.†

4. *Analogy* will not inform us. A small pivot or wheel cannot *infallibly* indicate to us the mechanism to which it belongs, nor anything conclusive as to whether the whole had only one or more makers. So of the universe, no part can shadow forth the whole of that, nor inform us conclusively whether it had a creator or creators. And here it is to be observed the difficulty is greater than with machines—for a pivot or wheel is a finite part of a

* *Oracle of Reason*, No. 31, p. 251.

† Since this time Mr. Francis William Newman has put this argument unanswerably in these words: 'A God uncaused and existing from eternity, is to the full as incomprehensible as a world uncaused and existing from eternity.'—'The Soul,' p. 36. Second edition.

finite whole, and *both comprehensible ;* but with the universe, all we can take cognisance of is but a very finite part of an *infinite* whole, and that whole to all men acknowledgedly *incomprehensible*. Moreover, *creation* can have no analogy — no one ever saw or can conceive of anything being created. So that this mode of learning the existence of a God fails. The Rev. Hugh M'Neile, M.A., minister of St. Jude's Church, Liverpool, in a lecture delivered to above four hundred of the Irish clergy, at the Rotunda in Dublin, said in reference to this part of the question, 'I am convinced, I say, that, from external creation, no right conclusion can be drawn concerning the *moral* character of God. Creation is too deeply and disastrously blotted in consequence of man's sin, to admit of any satisfactory result from an *adequate* contemplation of nature. The authors of a multitude of books on this subject, have given an inadequate and partial induction of particulars. Already aware (though perhaps scarcely recognising how or whence) that "God is love," they have looked on nature for proofs of this conclusion, and taken what suited their purpose. But they have not taken nature *as a whole*, and collected a conclusion fairly from impartial premises. They expatiate on the blessings and enjoyments of life, in the countless tribes of earth, air, and sea. But if life be a blessing, death is a curse. Nature presents the universal triumph of death. Is this the doing of a God of love ? or are there two Gods—a kind one, giving life ; and an unkind one taking it away; and the wicked one invariably the victor ? In external creation, exclusively and adequately contemplated, there is no escape from Manichæism. It is vain to say that the death of the inferior creatures is a blessing to man ; for why, in the creation of a God of love, should any such necessity exist ? And how would this account for the death of man himself ?' So far the argument of analogy.

5. *Revelation.*—We have *none.* If others ever had, we can only determine it by human reason, and for this purpose Leslie has furnished his well-known rules. Therefore, as revelation means something superadded to reason, we cannot be said to possess it, for reason has to determine what is, and what is not revelation, and therefore is superior to it. Also, it is contended by divines that, but for the Bible we should know nothing of a God, which shows the unsatisfactory nature of the four methods of learning his existence we have gone through. And Lord Brougham contends that but for natural theology, or the analogy argument, which has been shown to be no argument at all, the Bible would have no other basis than mere tradition.

So you see, gentlemen, the philosophical difficulties besetting the path of a young inquirer into sacred things. These difficulties are to me insuperable, and hence I find myself incapable of employing language you are more fortunate in being able to adapt to your conscience.*

But it has been stated I said I would put the Deity on half-pay. After first stating that I did not believe there was a Deity, is it likely I should say I would put him on half-pay? Would you put a servant on half-pay whom you never hired or had? All my expressions went to prove that I referred to the expenses of religion. I could not suppose that there is a being capable of governing the world, and consider him good and kind, and yet have any intention of bringing him into contempt. I had no personal reference to the Deity. I made use of that figure of speech because I thought they would understand it better, and they did understand it. I was saying we had many heavy burdens to pay to capitalists and others, and that I thought it hung like a millstone round us. Sir R. Peel said, when he introduced the income-tax, that the poor man could bear no more. I said there were twenty-four millions taken from us for the support of religion, and that they would do well to reduce that one-half. Suppose, gentlemen, that I did refer to the Deity, was my notion a dishonourable one? What man of you who had enough and to spare, and seeing the people around him in poverty, would not willingly relinquish part of his income to give them a bare subsistence? Who will deny that in England there are honest, industrious, hard-working men, honourable women, and beautiful children, who have not the means of obtaining food? Did I do him a disgrace if I thought he, who is called our Father, the Most High, would have dispensed with one-half of the lip-service he receives in order to give his creatures necessaries!

[It being nearly four o'clock the Jury asked leave to retire, to which Mr. Holyoake consenting, they left the Court for a short time. Some ladies who represented themselves as wives of clergymen, came round the dock offering Mr Holyoake confections and refreshment, and expressing their regret at the treatment he had received, and the position in which he was placed.]

Mr. Holyoake, on resuming, said—According to a calculation that has never been disputed, the

		Pay to their Clergy.
'Catholics, numbering...	124,672,000 ...	£6,106,000
Protestants ,,	54,046,000 ...	11,906,000

* The object of this passage was to show the jury the intellectual difficulties belonging to this subject, and the passage formed but an episode among the moral issues I raised. A friend of mine asking an eminent critic at one of Dr. Elliotson's seances, (who had read the report of the Trial) what he thought of my defence. 'Oh it turned upon that eternal *conundrum* the existence of God,' was the answer. But I hope the reader will see something more in my defence than the frivolity that employs itself on riddles.

Greek Church ,, ... 41,000,000 ...   760,000

Total of Christians 219,718,000   £18,762,000

'Of which England, for twenty-one millions of people, pays more than one-half.'* Thus the English pay five times more according to their numbers—I proposed a reduction of only one-half.

Mr. W. J. Fox has told us—'If the government of the country disposed of the mismanaged funds of the clergy, they would have sufficient for their annual needful expenditure.'

Mr. Justice Erskine. If you can convince the jury that your only meaning was that the incomes of the clergy ought to be reduced, and that you did not intend to insult God, I should tell the jury you ought not to be convicted. You need not go into a laboured defence of that.

Mr. Holyoake. It was stated by one of the witnesses at Cheltenham that I said Christians are worshippers of Mammon. I thought it necessary for me to refer to it.

Mr. Justice Erskine. There is no evidence of that.

Mr. Holyoake. Then turn to the question *What is blasphemy?* In the case of Mr. Southwell, one of the witnesses for the prosecution stated his opinion that the crime was '*bringing a scandal on the religion of the magistrates.*' Perhaps this is as correct a definition as can be given. It has been said to be 'an injury to God.' Men who could not string six sentences together grammatically, have told me they would defend God—men whom I should be ashamed to have defending me. But blasphemy is impossible in the sense of annoyance to God. Jonathan Edwards says—'The following things may be laid down as maxims of plain truth and indisputable evidence:—

'1. That God is a perfectly happy being, in the most absolute and highest sense possible.

'2. It will follow from hence, that God is free from everything that is *contrary to happiness*: and so that in strict propriety of speech there is no such thing as any pain, grief, or trouble in God.

'3. Where any intelligent being is really crossed and disappointed, and things are contrary to what he truly desires, he is less pleased, or has the less pleasure, his pleasure and happiness are diminished, and he suffers what is disagreeable to him, or is the subject of something that is of a nature contrary to joy and happiness, even pain and grief.

'From this last maxim it follows, that if no distinction is to be admitted between God's hatred of sin, and his will with respect to

* 'Cheap Salvation.' By Henry Hetherington.

the event and existence of sin, as the all-wise determiner of all events, under the view of all consequences through the whole compass and series of things; I say, then, it certainly follows, that the coming to pass of every individual act of sin is truly, all things considered, contrary to his will, and that his will is really crossed in it, and that in proportion as he hates it. And as God's hatred of sin is infinite, by reason of the infinite contrariety of his holy nature to sin; so his will is infinitely crossed in every act of sin that happens. Which is as much as to say:—he endures that which is infinitely disagreeable to him, by means of every act of sin he sees committed—and so he must be infinitely crossed and suffer infinite pain every day, in millions of millions of instances, which would be to make him infinitely the most miserable of all beings.'

But *blasphemy* is an antiquated accusation. In a work[†] by Col. Peyronnet Thompson, it is remarked—'what a turmoil, what a splutter, was in this land, when men first announced that they would not eat fish, they would not bow down, they would not confess but when they liked, and this because the secret had got wind that these things were either not in the priests' own rule, or were against it! What threats of hell flames, what splashing about of fire and brimstone, what registration of judgments on men choked with a beef-steak on Friday! Look at one of those simple men in the present day, who shock themselves with the barouches, the cigars, the newspapers, and the elephants of a London Sunday, and occasionally digress to Paris, for the keener excitation of seeing Punch upon the Boulevards, and wondering where heaven reserves its thunder. And put the parallel case, that a good Austrian or Navarrese Catholic came here, and grieved his heart with our weekly doings on a Friday, to say nothing of our more wholesale offences for forty days together in Lent. "Such frying; such barbecuing; in no place did I see anybody having the smallest notion of a red herring! All are involved in one flood of sin and gravy! How fathomless the patience of heaven, that such an island is not swallowed up of the deep!" We have looked into the rule he professes to go by; and we declare it is not there, but the contrary. We know we must appear in the next world with all our mutton on our heads. But we have done our best to look at the rule with the light that God has given us; and in spite of Austria or Navarre, we will take the risk of His not being

---

[*] Quoted from 'A Commentary on the Public Discussion on the subjects of Necessity and Responsibility,' &c. By Jonathan Jonathan, late of the United States.

[†] 'The Question of Sabbath Observance, tried by the Church's own rule,' &c. By Col. Peyronnet Thompson, F.R.S., of Queen's College, Cambridge.

angry with us, for seeing no prohibition of mutton there.' Thus we see that *mutton-eating* was at one period blasphemous.

Mr. Sergeant Talfourd told the jury, in the case of Hetherington *v.* Moxon, that if the government were consistent in carrying out prosecutions for blasphemy—Shakspere, Milton, Byron, Shelley, Southey—might be prohibited. This perhaps would be an agreeable result to a reverend gentleman well known in this court and county, who says all science should be destroyed; but I trust you entertain no such feelings, and that if I can show that my sentiments cannot be productive of harm, you will feel called upon to acquit me. I claim no inherent right of expressing my opinions, I only contend for liberty of expression because required for the public good. A doctrine was laid down by Lord John Russell upon the occasion of the presentation of the National Petition, which I will quote as a view of the subject of human rights well expressed.

'I am aware,' he said, 'that it is a doctrine frequently urged, and I perceive dwelt upon in this petition, that every male of a certain age has a right, absolute and inalienable, to elect a representative to take his place among the members in the Commons' House of Parliament. Now, sir, I never could understand that indefeasible right. It appears to me that that question, like every other in the practical application of politics, is to be settled by the institutions and the laws of the country of which the person is a native. I see no more right that a person twenty one years of age has to elect a member of parliament than he has to be a juryman. I conceive that you may just as well say that every adult male has a right to sit upon a jury to decide the most complicated and difficult questions of property, or that every man has a right to exercise the judicial functions, as the people did in some of the republics of antiquity. These things, as it appears to me, are not matters of right; but if it be for the good of the people at large, if it be conducive to the right government of the state, if it tend to the maintenance of the freedom and welfare of the people, that a certain number, defined and limited by a reference to a fixed standard of property, should have the right of electing members of parliament, and if it be disadvantageous to the community at large that the right of suffrage should be universal, then I say that on such a subject the consideration of the public good should prevail, that legislation must act upon it as on every other, and that no inalienable right can be quoted against that which the good of the whole demands.'

If Lord Russell did not, I do see a difference between the claim of an elector and the right of a juryman. The elector is chiefly concerned with his own interests, the juryman with other people's—one is simple, the other complex. But with the measure of right laid down by his lordship in the sentiments I have quoted, I perfectly accord, and if it could be shown that freedom of expression produced public harm, then I would give it up. But I believe such a right would produce good, and therefore I claim it at your hands upon the ground of public good.

In what I urge, it is not faith but reason, as far as I understand it, that I take for my guide—a rule of argument I trust you will accept. 'Reason contents me,' was inscribed as the motto on the seal of the letter from Sir James Graham, acknowledging the receipt of the Cheltenham memorial. If reason 'contents' the Secretary of State, and 'fountain of justice,' surely it ought to 'content' the channels through which such justice is diffused over society. Reason would always be preferred by us were we not differently instructed. 'Bewildered,' says Diderot, 'in an immense forest during the night, and having only one small torch for my guide, a stranger approaches and thus addresses me: "*Friend, blow out thy light if thou wouldst make sure of the right path.*" The "forest" was the world—the "light" was my reason—the "stranger" was a priest.'

After several quotations showing the dubious and often pernicious influence of sacred authority, Mr. Holyoake observed—Religious sanctions are regarded only by the ignorant, whom they confirm in folly. The good find their sanction in the satisfaction of a virtuous act performed. In an address of the Rev. F. Close, delivered a short time since at the Church of England Tradesmen and Working Men's Association of Cheltenham, he said, 'that the more a man is advanced in human knowledge, the more is he opposed to religion, and the more deadly enemy he is to the truth of God.' If this Christian minister is to be believed, then may you burn your books—forsake all mental refinement—and be equal in piety and ignorance. If Christianity is opposed to human improvement, then should all systems of ignorance be patronised by Christians. Sentiments like these would lead us to give up Boyle, Locke, and Newton, and regard them, with the Rev. Mr. Close, with detestation.

Mr. Justice Erskine. Let me see the discourse of Mr. Close from which you are quoting.

The book was handed to his lordship.

Mr. Holyoake. If the correctness of that report be doubted, I may state that the sentiments of Mr. Close were replied to by Mr. G. Berkeley.

Permit me now to draw your attention strongly to what has been said by men in authority of the impolicy of these prosecutions—that even if you were justified in inflicting punishment on me, it would not be wise to do so. Lord Brougham, three or four years ago, said, 'I may underrate the power of truth opposed to error, and I may overrate the good sense of my fellow countrymen in rejecting it, but one thing I do not overrate—the power of persecution to spread that which persecution only can spread.' When I walk through any of those ancient places, as I did yesterday through your beautiful cathedral, I feel the majesty they ever present, and think of the manner in which our Catholic ancestors acted on the minds of men. There were sublimity and pageantry and pomp to create awe. We have none now of that beauty of architecture in our meagre churches and more meagre chapels. They had a service more imposing than we ever had. Recollecting all these things, I have wondered how anything could be found sufficiently powerful to shake them off. I have wondered how Luther, with his rude vulgarity, could have effected so much. I can only account for it in this way—that when the Catholics dragged his followers to gaol, it was found that human feelings were stronger than human creeds.

These prosecutions are entirely in opposition to the sentiments promulgated by yourselves, as appears from a book given me in gaol called the 'Manual of Devotion.' I amused myself by contrasting the profession contained in it with the practice of my opponents. It is published by the 'Society for Promoting Christian Knowledge.' In the 'Discourse concerning Prayer,' it is laid down that the 'second qualification for prayer is charity or love. There is nothing so contrary to the nature of God, nothing so wide of the true spirit of a Christian, as bitterness and wrath, malice and envy; and therefore it is vain to think that even our prayers can be acceptable to God, till we have put on, as the elect of God, bowels of mercy, kindness, humbleness of mind, meekness, long-suffering, forbearing one another, and forgiving one another, as St. Paul commands.' Gentlemen, where are these sentiments evinced in this prosecution?

The 'third qualification—Is faith. If any of you lack wisdom, says St. James, let him ask of God, but let him ask in faith.' My prosecutors have asked Mr. Bubb, have had faith in policemen, and confidence only in the 'common law.'

The 'fourth qualification is—That in all things of a temporal concern, we must exercise an entire submission to the will of God. A good Christian will be sure to leave the issue in God's hands.' In my case not the will of God, but the will of bigots was done, and the 'issue' left in the turnkey's hands.

The 'fifth qualification—Is that the person praying hath a good intention; that he asks for a good end. We must not pray as the revengeful man when he prays for authority, that he may have the more power to effect his evil designs.' What can be more wholly condemnatory of these proceedings than these instructions of the 'Manual of Devotion?'

When the 'Life of Christ,' by Dr. Strauss, appeared in Berlin, contrary to usages in such matters, the Prussian government consulted the clergy to ascertain from them whether it would not be prudent to prohibit this extraordinary production. The celebrated Bishop Neander was commissioned by the ecclesiastical body of Berlin, to peruse the book and to return an answer. Neander did so, and declared in reply, that the work submitted to his examination threatened, it was true, the demolition of all creeds; nevertheless, he requested that full liberty should not be denied to his adversary, in order that full and free discussion might be the only judges between truth and error. And when asked whether it should be prosecuted, said, 'No, I will answer it.'

Mr. Justice Erskine. That work was temperately written.

Mr. Holyoake. Neander did reply to it, and Strauss had the manliness to acknowledge that it had corrected many of his errors. Would that have been done had he been prosecuted? Dr. Strauss's work on the scriptures got him a professor's chair in Germany. In this country it would have made him amenable to the common law, and to one, two, or three years' imprisonment.

Gentlemen, in the pertinacity of my open reply to Maitland, you may find something objectionable, but I happen to be an admirer of that sentiment expressed by the honest 'Vicar of Wakefield'—'In all human institutions a smaller evil is allowed to procure a greater good; as in politics, a province may be given away, to secure a kingdom; in medicine, a limb may be lopt off, to preserve the body. But in religion, the law is written and inflexible, *never* to do evil.' Then, gentlemen, I ought to be tolerated in the truthfulness of my answer. Milton, in his Prose Works,* in reference to an incident in his travels, says:—

'While I was on my way back to Rome, some merchants informed me that the English Jesuits had formed a plot against me, if I returned to Rome, because I had spoken too freely of religion; for it was a rule which I laid down to myself in those places, never to be the first to begin any conversation on religion—but, if any questions were put to me concerning my faith, to declare it without any reserve or fear.'

This is the rule which I myself have followed in this case.

Since his lordship—with more liberality than is customary, and with more philosophy than I expected on matters of religion (on which I hear his lordship thinks very devoutly)—has said, that any religion may be discussed in temperate language, it is not

---

* Milton's Prose Works, pp. 933-4, 8vo edit. Edited by Fletcher.

necessary for me to prove, as I should have done, that it would be useless liberty for me to entertain opinions without permission to publish them. The only question is whether, in the expression of these opinions, I used a proper kind of language. I think I have proved that I was far from having any of those 'malicious' feelings the indictment presupposes. Many figures of speech have been used in this court from which my feelings revolted as much as those of any person could from what I said. No allowance is made for this, and too much importance is attached to what is assumed to be ridicule. A short time ago it was argued, that if the political squibs which are seen in shop windows were permitted to be published, they would bring government into contempt, and you would soon have no government. Their publication has been permitted. Have we no government now? I feel the utility of a government, and no force of ridicule could shake my belief in the importance of good government. So it is with religion. Nothing that is uttered, however contemptuous, can bring it into contempt, if it really is useful and beneficial. We might defy all the wits and caricaturists in the world to bring the problems of Euclid into contempt. No man can bring into contempt that which is essential and true.

The counsel who opened the case did not state whether the indictment was at statute or common law.

Mr. Justice Erskine. Common law.

Mr. Holyoake. Then, gentleman of the jury, I shall draw your attention to that, and I hope I shall be able to explain the law bearing on my case.

Mr. Justice Erskine. The jury must take the law from me. I am responsible for that.

Mr. Holyoake. I know, my lord; but still I may refer to it. A friend of mine consulted the works bearing upon the law of this case.* I have here the results of his labours, and, if I am wrong, your lordship will, in summing up, correct me.

Gentleman of the jury, the common law is a judge-made law. A judge laid down, some years ago, that to say anything against the Christian religion was an indictable offence. Another judge followed him and said the same; and at last it came not to be doubted. If I show there is no law properly made in parliament assembled, you ought to acquit me.

The offence with which I am charged is an offence at common law. There is no statute which punishes a man simply for denying the existence of God. There is a statute (9 and 10 Wm. III., c. 32) directed against those who denied the Trinity and who re-

* I was indebted to Mr. J. Humffreys Parry, barrister, for the revision of the argument I employed.

nounced Christianity. But the former part has been repealed, in favour of Unitarians, by the 53rd Geo. III., c. 160; and the words I am charged with having spoken cannot be brought within the latter. There is a statute against profane cursing and swearing (19 Geo. II., c. 21), but it takes no cognisance of this offence. Human beings have also been put to death for witchcraft (33 Hen. VIII., c. 8; and 1 James I., c. 12), under the merciless statutes which were enacted in times of the grossest ignorance and superstition; but those statutes have been repealed (9 Geo. II., c. 5). This offence, therefore, is an offence against the common law, if it is an offence at all. It is to be found in the recorded decisions of the judges, if it is to be found anywhere; and the punishment for it is in their discretion. Had it been an offence under a statute, it would have been impossible for me to have denied the authority of the statute; but, as it is an offence at common law, it is quite competent for me to show that the authorities which have been supposed to constitute the offence do not warrant such a construction. Should your lordship even declare that you had no doubt upon the subject, it would still be competent for me to bring before you the decisions of former judges, to argue upon those decisions, and to show, if I could, that there was some mistake or error running throughout the whole of them. Your lordship, I am sure, will admit that judges are fallible, and that a blind, unreasoning submission to them no man should give. As some excuse for presuming to doubt the decision of some of your lordship's predecessors, I shall quote the following passage from the preface to Mr. Watkin's treatise on Conveyancing, allowed to be a master-piece of legal sagacity and method. 'I believe,' writes that gentleman, 'it will be found, on examination, that an implicit submission to the assertions of our predecessors, whatever station those predecessors may have held, has been one of the most certain sources of error, Perhaps there is nothing which has so much shackled the human intellect, nothing which has so greatly promoted whatever is tyrannic, preposterous, and absurd, nothing perhaps which has so much degraded the species in the scale of being as the implicit submission to individual dicta.' And he then goes on in vigorous terms to reprobate the practice of allowing 'authority to shoulder out common sense, or adhering to precedent in defiance of principle.' Upon the principle contained in this passage I shall act, in claiming the attention of your lordship, and you, gentlemen of the jury, whilst I examine the authorities for the doctrine which brings the offence with which I am charged within the jurisdiction of the temporal courts. Your lordship will, perhaps, refer to these books.

Mr. Justice Erskine. No need of that. If it is not an offence at common law, this indictment is worth nothing. You can take it before the fifteen judges on a writ of error. I sit here, not to correct the law, but merely to administer it.*

Mr. Holyoake resumed. In the fourth volume of 'Blackstone's Commentaries,' p. 59, in speaking of offences against God and religion, that writer says, 'The fourth species of offences, therefore, more immediately against God and religion, is that of blasphemy against the Almighty, by denying his being or providence, or by contumelious reproaches of our saviour, Christ. Whither also may be referred all profane scoffing at the holy scripture, or exposing it to contempt and ridicule. These are offences punishable at common law by fine and imprisonment, or other infamous corporal punishment; *for Christianity is part of the laws of England.*' Blackstone quotes, in support of the first species, a volume of 'Ventris' Reports,' p. 298; and the second from the second volume of 'Strange's Reports,' p. 834. Mr. Christian, the commentator upon Blackstone, adds, in a note, a passage from the 'Year Book' (34 Henry VI.), folio 43.

The earliest case is that from the year book, in the 34th year of Henry VI. (1458). Mr. Christian quotes from it this passage—'Scripture est common ley, sur quel toutes manieres de leis sont fondes' (*i.e.*, Scripture is common law, upon which all descriptions of laws are founded). Were this quotation correct, and did the word scripture here mean 'holy scripture,' or what is generally understood by the Bible, then I admit this passage would be a good foundation to build up Mr. Judge Blackstone's law. But it is no such thing. The case in the year book is a case of *quare impedit*, and, in the course of the argument the question arose whether, in a matter of induction to a benefice by the ordinary (*i.e.*, the bishop) the common law would take notice of, or be bound by, the law or practices of the church. Whereupon, Chief Justice Prisot says—'To such laws, which they of the holy church have in "ancient writing," it becomes us to give credence, for such is common law, upon which all descriptions of laws are founded. And therefore, sir, we are obliged to recognise their law of the holy church—likewise they are obliged to recognise our law. And, sir, if it appears to us now that the bishop has done as an ordinary should do in such a case, then we ought to judge it good—if otherwise, bad.'

In this passage, then, there is not one word about scripture in the sense of 'holy scripture.' Judge Prisot says, 'To such laws

* I have been told by a legal friend of great experience, that at this point I might have taken the judge at his word, and have carried the case before the judges for decision; but I was unacquainted with the forms of law in such cases, and I moreover distrusted the judge.

as the church has in ancien scripture (*i. e.*, ancient writing) we ought to give credence.' And what does he mean by 'laws which the church has in ancient writing?' not any laws that are to be found in the Bible, but the canon or ecclesiastical laws by which the temporal concerns of the church are guided. And the reason he uses the phrase 'ancien scripture,' or ancient writing, is that the laws were not then printed; the only record of them was in writing. Printing had not been introduced into England, and was only just discovered on the continent, the laws therefore of the spiritual and temporal courts were only to be seen in writing. And as though there should be no doubt as to his meaning, he goes on to say, 'And as we are obliged to recognise their laws (that is the ecclesiastical laws, or laws of the spiritual courts), so they are obliged to recognise our laws (that is, the laws of the temporal courts).' It must therefore be evident that this quotation of Mr. Christian is a perversion or mistake, a judicial forgery or a judicial blunder, and in either case its authority is of no value. It must be dismissed altogether from our minds in considering what the law is upon this point—that is, whether Christianity is or is not a part and parcel of the law of England. Unfortunately, however, we shall find that this case is actually made the substratum of the law. In proving, therefore, that it cannot warrant such a law, surely I prove that at common law, at least to speak against Christianity, is not an offence.

The next case is that in Ventris' Report, vol. 1, p. 293. It is called Taylor's case, and Chief Justice Hale certainly declares explicitly in this case, 'that Christianity is parcel of the laws of England.' But he cites no authority whatever.

In the case analysed from the year book, it is expressly said, that the common law is to be found in 'ancient writings,' and the unsupported dictum of a judge in the middle of the seventeenth century cannot be construed as a part of the ancient writings of the common law. Either the law already existed or it did not. If it did, the question is—where is it? If it did not, Chief Justice Hale could not then make it for the first time; and this case in Ventris' cannot be said to lay down the law. The case in the second volume of Strange is the King *v.* Woolston. The defendant had been convicted of writing four blasphemous discourses against the divinity and character of Christ; and upon attempting to move in arrest of judgment, the court declared they would not suffer it to be debated whether to write against Christianity in general was an offence punishable in the temporal courts of common law. And they cited Taylor's case, which has been shown to be an insufficient authority, or rather no authority at all, and the King *v.* Hale, in the same volume of Strange, p.

416, but which was an indictment under the statute (9 & 10 Wm. III.) for speaking against the Trinity, and therefore cannot in any way support the common law doctrine.

The first person who called attention to the utter want of authority in the common law for the dictum 'that Christianity was part of the common law,' was Jefferson, the second president of America—himself a profound lawyer, and to his references I am indebted for the foregoing authorities, which, however, have been carefully verified. Mr. Jefferson, in a letter to Major Cartwright, to be found in vol. ii., p. 272, of his 'Memoirs,' exposes the mode in which this law was created. Alluding to the case of Prisot, he says, 'Finch in his first book, c. 3, is the first who afterwards quotes this case. He misstates it thus: "To such laws of the church as have warrant in holy scripture, our law giveth credence," and cites Prisot, mistranslating "ancien scripture" into holy scripture. This was in 1613, a century and a half after the dictum of Prisot. Wingate, in 1658, erects this false translation into a maxim of the common law, copying the words of Finch, but citing Prisot. Shephard, title "Religion," in 1675, copies the same mistranslation, quoting the year book, Finch, and Wingate. Hale expresses it in these words, "Christianity is parcel of the laws of England," but quotes no authority. Wood, 409, ventures still to vary the phrase, and says, "that all blasphemy and prophaneness are offences by the common law," and Blackstone repeats the words of Hale.' In the case of the the King *v.* Carlile, decided since Mr. Jefferson wrote this letter, there was no argument as to the common law. The question was as to whether the statute (9 & 10 Wm. III.) had superseded the common law. But the common law itself was not called in question, which I submit it should be, and by a wise example superseded.

But let us see what Christianity is according to common law? We may remark—

1. Its inconsistency.—It calls blasphemy the greatest crime man can commit. Yet in the case of Hetherington *v.* Moxon, it permits the *respectable* blasphemer to go free. Blasphemy in guinea volumes it allows, but exhibits the holiest horror at it when in penny pamphlets.

2. Its barbarity, as in Peter Annet's case.—In Michaelmas term, M. 3. G. 3. Peter Annet was convicted on an information for writing 'a most blasphemous libel,' in weekly papers called the *Free Inquirer*, to which he pleaded guilty; in consideration of which, and of his poverty, of his having confessed his errors in an affidavit, and of his being 74 years old, and some symptoms of wildness that appeared on his inspection in court, the court

declared they had mitigated his punishment to the following : To be imprisoned in Newgate for one month ; to stand twice in the pillory with a paper on his forehead, inscribed Blasphemy ; to be sent to the House of Correction to hard labour for a year ; to pay a fine of 6s. 8d., and to find security himself in £100, and two sureties in £50 each for his good behaviour during life.*

3. *Its capriciousness.*—The common law before the time of Henry VIII. was one thing, but afterwards it was another. The language which was blasphemy at the first period, was not so in the other. Those expressions which insulted God before Henry the Eighth was born, did not insult him afterwards. Henry the Eighth's opinion made the difference. Lord Commissioner Whitelocke (5 Howell's State Trials, p. 826), in Debate whether James Nayler the quaker should suffer death, remarked, ' I remember a case in our book H. 7, where the bishop committed one to prison for a heretic, and the heresy was denying " that tythes were due to the parson." This at that time was a very great heresy.'

4. *Its disregard of equal justice.*—A British subject would be punished for firing into a Turkish vessel; but he is not punishable for attacking the captain and sailors with Bibles and tracts, which, if they read and believe, will make them apostates from the faith of Mahomet, and blasphemers of the Koran. While on terms of amity with the Sublime Porte, the laws of England restrain us from despoiling them of their property, but not from despoiling them of their religion.†

5. *It debases religion as best set forth.*—' Religion (says Miss Martineau) is, in its widest sense, " the tendency of human nature to the infinite ;" and its principle is manifested in the pursuit of perfection in any direction whatever. It is in this widest sense that some speculative atheists have been religious men ; religious in their efforts after self-perfection ; though unable to personify their conception of the infinite. In a somewhat narrower sense, religion is the relation which the highest human sentiments bear towards an infinitely perfect being. There can be no further narrowing than this. Any account of religion which restricts it within the boundaries of any system, which connects it with any mode of belief, which implicates it with hope of reward, or fear of punishment, is low and injurious, and debases religion into superstition.' How much more is religion degraded that is made the subject of reward and punishment here ?

Thus speaks the common law upon these points; and thus, as

---

* Blackstone's Reports, p. 395.

† Vide *Freethinker's Information for the People.*

part of the common law, speaks Christianity. Will you, by a verdict of guilty this day, send forth to the world this card of credentials of the religion of Jesus?

The intention of a libel constitutes its criminality. It is for you, gentlemen, to say whether I knowingly, wickedly, and maliciously offended the law ? Malice is necessary to a libel—conscientious words are allowable.

'Contumely and contempt are what no establishment can tolerate: but on the other hand it would not be proper to lay any restraint upon rational and dispassionate discussions of the rectitude and propriety of the established mode of worship.' 4 Bla. Com. 51; 1 Pmp. 219. And Mr. Starkie, on the subject, says 'that it may not be going too far from the principles and decisions, that no author or preacher who fairly and conscientiously promulgates the opinions with whose truth he is impressed for the benefit of others, is for so doing amenable as a criminal, that a malicious and mischievous intention is in such case the broad boundary between right and wrong; and that if it can be collected from the offensive levity with which so serious a subject is treated, or from other circumstances, that the act of the party was malicious, then, since the law has no means of distinguishing between different degrees of evil tendency, if the matter published contain any such tendency, the publisher becomes amenable to justice.'*

As to the duty of the jury, I have Lord Chief Justice Abbott's opinion, in his charge to the jury in summing up the evidence against Mr. Joseph Russell at the Warwick Summer Assizes, on Friday, August 13, 1819, for a political libel, being Mr. Hone's 'Parody on the Litany.' Mr. Russell argued that as Hone had been acquitted for publishing it, he also ought to be. 'No one,' says his lordship, ' is more inclined than myself to speak reverently of the decision of juries. But, gentlemen, you cannot, under the sanction of an oath, take the verdict of those juries either directly or indirectly as your guide in the verdict you are called upon to give in this case. Those juries, no doubt, returned their verdicts honestly and conscientiously according to the evidence that was layed before them. What that evidence was you can know nothing of. You are to try the question by your own consciences and by your own reason. They might have been right in their decision, and you should be careful that you are right in yours.'

After this, you will see it is clear that though a jury had before found a person guilty of the offence I am charged with, it will be no justification of your doing so too. [Here Mr. Holyoake, perceiving that he would be heard fairly, and that no attempts to put him down were practised, laid aside a handful of notes, and said]

* Starkie on Libel, pp. 496-7.

—I have to thank your lordship, and you, gentlemen of the jury, for the courtesy and attention with which I have been heard. Gentlemen, if I have occupied you long you will find my apology in the circumstance that your verdict against me will occupy me longer. I could wish that justice to me and your convenience had permitted brevity. The length of my defence has originated with the charge against me, and not with myself.

It is said, that when Southey was asked if he were not ashamed of having written *Wat Tyler*, he answered, no more ashamed than I am of having been young. Meaning, any man may err in youth. So I erred in being religious in my early days. If I am not religious now, deem me not criminal. Religion never did me a service, how then should I love it? But it assailed my youth with gloomy dogmas, now it assails my liberty.

Gentlemen, if during my address to you I have offended by the frankness of my avowals, it has not proceeded from a disregard of your feelings, but from the belief that, as men, you would prefer independence to servility of speech.

Of the nature of the charge against me I add no further word. My only crime has been the discharge of what I considered a duty. For my difference in opinion with you upon the question of Deity, I offer no apology. I have made no contract to think as you do, and I owe you no obligation to do it. If I commanded you to abjure your belief, you would disregard it as impertinence, and if you punish me for not adjuring mine, how will you reconcile it with 'doing as you would wish to be done unto?'

Had I said, that there is no God, still I should not deserve the penalties of the law. If I point to the wrong I see in this Christian country, and ask, is this Christianity? you would reply, ' No; what you refer to results from men who live without God in the world.' Then, gentlemen, would you punish me for simply saying that which other men, unpunished, are every day doing?

If I have said that religious revenues should be reduced one half, I spoke only the dictates of humanity at this season of national suffering. Surely it is not blasphemous to argue that human misery should be alleviated at the expense of spiritual pride.

I ask not equal rights with yourselves. You, as Christians, can imprison those who differ from you. I do not offend your pride by asking to be admitted your equals here. I desire not such privileges. I claim merely the right to speak my convictions; to show a man the right path when I think he takes the wrong one.

It is a melancholy maxim in these courts of law, that the greater the truth the greater the libel; and so it would be with me this day could I demonstrate to you that there is no Deity. The more correct I am the severer would be my punishment, because the law regards the belief in a God to be the foundation of obedience among men. But I trust I have convinced you that my views of this question are compatible with the practice of all our duties to our fellow-men, borne out by eminent authority and long experience.

Setting aside the reprobation of persecution by Middleton, by Clarke, by Latimer, and other divines I have quoted; Leslie, Reid, and Bulwer have contended that the objections of the sceptic merely strengthen the fabric of piety they pretend to assail. Gentlemen, which is to be believed, divines and philosophers, or the common law? These persons speak as though they believed Christianity to be true; the common law punishes as though it knew it to be false.

If the state religion be true, my opinion can never overcome it; and by convicting me you publish your consciousness of error in the cause you are placed there to defend as truth. If God be truth you libel him and his power, and publish the omnipotence of error.

When in gaol, I one day opened the rules drawn up by the judges. The 167th opens thus: 'No prisoner shall lie.' Now, gentlemen, how is a man to act under these circumstances in which I am placed? If you find me guilty upon the indictment before you, my case stands in this manner:—if I do not lie you imprison me, and if I do you punish me. Turning back to the morality of ancient days, and meditating with delight on their noble sincerity and love of truth, am I to count it a misfortune to live in modern times and among a Christian people?

In your churches, as I have read to you, you implore that truth and justice may descend among men, and the supplication is a noble one. Gentlemen, will you pray for truth in your churches and brand it in your courts?

The atmosphere of your gaols as little assimilates with my taste as their punishments will accord with my constitution. I seek not these things, I assure you, but when they lie in the path o duty I trust I shall ever prefer them to a dereliction from it.

But, gentlemen, supposing that they are my sentiments that you are requested to punish; you should first do yourselves the justice to reflect what has been said about them and insinuated in this court. Learned divines, and sage writers on atheism, agree that it is too absurd to need refutation—too barren to satisfy, too monstrous to attract, too fearful to allure, too dumb to speak, and too deathly not to appal its own votaries. It is styled too grave to entertain youth, and too devoid of consolation for the trembling wants of age—too abstract for the comprehension of the ignorant, and too unreasonable to gain the admiration of the intelligent. That it is alarming to the timid, and disquieting to the brave— that it negatives everything, and sets up nothing, and is so purely speculative that it can never have a practical bearing on the business of life. Gentlemen, will you disturb the harmony of these conclusions by a verdict against me, and attack that which never existed, and place upon the grave records of this court a slaying of the self-slain? Will you thus draw attention to a subject you perhaps think had better be forgotten, and create a conviction that it must be a greatly important one, since you erect it into public notice by directing the thunders of the law at young and comparatively inexperienced believer in its principl.?

Would you test my opinions by my emotions on the bed of death? Let me assure you, that if men can expect to die in peace who can send their fellow men to a gaol because of honest difference of opinion, I have nothing to fear.

I am told I may hold opinions, but must keep them to myself —which means, I may know and feel what is right, but must never do it. I must see my fellow-men in error, but never put them right. Must live every day below the standard of right my sense of duty and conscience sets up, and all my life long 'prove all things' and never 'hold fast to the good.'

The indictment charges me with having 'wickedly, maliciously, and with evil design,' against the peace of the Queen, uttered certain words. What shadow of evidence has been adduced to substantiate this extravagant charge?

Will you suffer this court to proclaim the sacred nature of an oath, and openly violate it in the same hour and under the same roof? I might ask in the spirit of that Christianity you sit there to administer, how do you propose to answer to your God in that day when the secrets of all hearts are to be opened, when all dissembling is to be exposed, and all perjury punished; how do you propose to answer for having invoked the name of God in this assembly only to disregard it, on the poor plea of precedent— that others have done so before? For, gentlemen, there is nothing else that even the subtlest sophistry can conjure up to justify you. But I best prefer appealing to you as honest men, in the spirit of my own reasoning, and thinking; as men with an eye to the improvement of mankind, who would break the unjust shackles that bind them, who would discard prejudice in order to be just, who will not condemn me because I am not rich, and who will listen to humanity rather than to bigotry, and respect truthfulness wherever you may find it. I believe that in every honest heart there is a sense of rectitude that rises superior to creeds, that respects all virtue and protects all truth, that asks for no names and seeks no precedents before resolving to do rightly, that fears no man's frowns, and dares to be just without custom's permit. To this feeling, gentlemen, only do I appeal, and by its verdict I am willing to abide.

Mr Justice Erskine: Gentlemen of the jury, although the lengthened address of the defendant has demanded from you so long endurance, in this vitiated atmosphere, I still trust we shall have enough of power left to direct our minds to the parts of this case which are important. The greater part of the time has been wasted on subjects with which you have nothing to do. We are not sitting here as a deliberative assembly to consider whether in respect of such cases as this it is politic or wise to imprison for opinions—whether men ought to be punished for uttering such sentiments—and I shall have nothing to say to you on that point. We have to decide on the law as we find it. I shall make no law—the judges made no law, but have handed it down from the earliest ages. I should have no more power to alter this than to say the eldest son is not the heir of his father. Allusion has been made to some expressions of mine, when in the course of my duty I directed the attention of the grand jury to these cases. Certainly the printed report was highly incorrect. I said nothing to prejudice them. Inasmuch as this offence directly tended to take away that foundation on which real morality can alone be safely based, I told them what I feel, that without religion there is no morality. I recommended that that foundation may be made by early education and habits of thought, but in so doing I did not mean to prejudge, nor do I seem to have been considered as doing so. I am not going to lay down as law that no man has a right to entertain opinions opposed to the religion of the state, nor to express them. Man is only responsible for his opinions to God, because God only can judge of his motives, and we arrogate his duties if we judge of men's sentiments. If men will entertain sentiments opposed to the religion of the state we require that they shall express them reverently, and philosophers who have discussed this subject all agree that this is right. Mr. Archdeacon Paley has stated this in language so plain, far better than any words I could supply myself. 'Serious arguments are fair on all sides. Christianity is but ill-defended by refusing audience or toleration to the objections of unbelievers. But whilst we would have freedom of inquiry restrained by no laws but those of decency, we are entitled to demand, on behalf of a religion which holds forth to mankind assurances of immortality, that its credit be assailed by no other weapons than those of sober discussion and legitimate reasoning.' Our law has adopted that as its rule, and men are not permitted to make use of indecent language in reference to God and the Christian religion, without rendering themselves liable to punishment. You have had a great number of books read to you, arguing whether it was politic to prosecute in such cases. One of the sentiments was a dignitary's reply, ' I will answer it.' That points out the difference in these cases.

Sober argument you may answer, but indecent reviling you cannot and therefore the law steps in and punishes it. You have been told you have to consider what is blasphemy. He asked the witness what he considered blasphemy, and he gave him a very sensible answer. What you have to try is, whether the defendant wickedly and devisedly did intend to bring the Christian religion into contempt among the people, by uttering words of and concerning Almighty God, the holy Scriptures, and the Christian religion. The charge is, that he uttered these words with the intention of bringing Almighty God, the Christian religion, and the holy Scriptures, into contempt. You are not called upon to say whether in your judgment the opinions of the defendant are right or wrong—whether it is right or wrong that words like these should be punished, but whether he uttered these words with the intent charged in the indictment. These words were proved by a witness who admits that others were used, that they did not follow consecutively, and that other words were interspersed. It is right that you should have the whole set before you, for a man is not to be judged for what is partly set before you, and therefore it was necessary you should have the whole of what was said. The way in which the witness related the statements made by defendant was this: He said he had been lecturing on 'Home Colonisation, Emigration, and Poor-Laws superseded.' After the lecture had been closed, some man whose name he did not then know, said the lecturer had been speaking of our duty to our fellow-men, but he had not spoken of our duty to our God, and it is important that you should notice that the words were not the subject of the lecture, but uttered in answer to a question put to him. There is no evidence that he intended to have said anything—there is no evidence that this person is a friend of the other person, or that this question was asked so as to give him an opportunity of uttering these sentiments.* If that had been the case it would have made it worse than if he had introduced it. This challenge having been made by this person, whoever it was, the defendant said—'I am of no religion at all; I do not believe in such a thing as a God.' There is nothing in the introduction of the word 'thing' to show that he intended to treat the subject with levity and contempt. You might take it that he said he did not believe there is such a being as a God. The witness went on: 'He said the people of this country are too poor to have any religion, he would serve the Deity as the government did the subaltern officers—place him on half-pay; I was

---

* The artifice which Mr. Justice Erskine here suggested to the jury never entered into my imagination. The evidence could not have given the jury any such idea, and I was pained and astonished to hear the judge employ it.

near the door; you said the reason was the expense of religion. And then he was asked as to his opinion of blasphemy. He is then cross-examined as to his knowledge of some report made by another person. 'You did not lay any emphasis on the word thing; you said the word in the ordinary tone of voice.' There is something which defendant has alleged himself to have stated* which gives a stronger sting than that which was given by the witness—'I flee the Bible as a viper.' The question is whether these words were uttered with the intention of bringing God and the Christian religion into contempt. Then the charge is made out, for I tell you that it is an offence at common law. If it is not an offence, the indictment is not worth the parchment it is written upon—if there is no such authority as that which I have laid down. Any man who treats with contempt the Christian religion, is guilty of an indictable misdemeanour. You have to consider the language and a passage read to you from a charge of a learned judge. 'It may not be going too far to state, that no author or preacher is forbidden stating his opinions sincerely. By maliciously is not meant malice against any particular individual, but a mischievous intent. This is the criterion, and it is a fair criterion, if it can be collected from the offensive levity in which the subject is treated, if the matter placed in the indictment contains any such tendency.' If the words had appeared in the course of a written paper you would have entertained no doubt that the person who had uttered these words had uttered them with levity. The only thing in his favour is, that it was not a written answer. The solution given by the defendant is, that although his opinions are unhappily such that he has no belief in a God, he had no intention of bringing religion into contempt. He went on to state that he considered it the duty of the clergymen of the establishment to have reduced their incomes one-half. If he had meant this, he ought to have made use of other language. You will dismiss from your minds all statements in newspapers, or other statements made out of court, and consider it in reference to the evidence. If you are convinced that he uttered it with levity, for the purpose of treating with contempt the majesty of Almighty God, he is guilty of the offence. If you think he made use of these words in the heat of argument without any such intent, you will give him the benefit of the doubt. If you are convinced that he did it with that object you must find him guilty, despite of all that has been addressed to you. If you entertain a reasonable doubt of his intention, you will give him the benefit of it.

* In the report of my original speech to Maitland, which I read to the court from the *Oracle*.

The jury, after a very brief deliberation, returned a verdict of *Guilty*.

[One of the jury was a Deist, a professed friend of free speech, and who had said that he never could convict me, but he wanted courage when the hour of the verdict came, and gave in against me. For myself, I never for a moment expected an acquittal. During the few moments of the jury's consultation, I took my watch from my neck and gave it, with my keys, to my friend, Mr. Knight Hunt. My papers I consigned to my friend Mr. W. B. Smith, as for all I knew they might the next moment become the property of the court by virtue of the sentence.]

Mr. Justice Erskine. George Jacob Holyoake, if you had been convicted as the author of that paper which Adams has been convicted of publishing, my sentence must have been very severe. But, although the name is the same, there is no evidence of it.* You have been convicted of uttering language, and although you have been adducing long arguments to show the impolicy of these prosecutions, you are convicted of having uttered these words with improper levity. The arm of the law is not stretched out to protect the character of the Almighty; we do not assume to be the protectors of our God, but to protect the people from such indecent language. And if these words had been written for deliberate circulation, I should have passed on you a severer sentence. You uttered them in consequence of a question—I have no evidence that this question was put to draw out these words. Proceeding on the evidence that has been given, trusting that these words have been uttered in the heat of the moment, I shall think it sufficient to sentence you to be *imprisoned in the Common Gaol for Six calendar months*.

Mr. Holyoake. My lord, am I to be classed with thieves and felons?

Mr. Justice Erskine. No; thieves and felons are sentenced to the Penitentiary, you to the Common Gaol.

The court adjourned at ten o'clock.

What was advanced by the counsel and the judge has been rendered in full in the foregoing report, but I have contented myself with an abstract of what I urged myself. The *Times* said I quoted from more than thirty authors, which is very

---

* This is another of those unwarranted suppositions in which the judge ought not to have indulged. 'That paper' was written by my friend Mr. Chilton, Editor of the *Oracle* in my absence, and signed with his initials. The judge might have known that I was in Gloucester Gaol when it was written and published. I should have stopped the judge and corrected him, but I feared by seeming to separate myself from Adams, to be thought capable of saving myself at his expense, or exposing him to new rigour.

likely; but it was not because I was not sensible of the good taste of brevity that I occupied the bench so long. I was standing that day in court fourteen hours, and, including the cross examinations, I was speaking more than eleven hours. I prepared notes to last me two days; and after the first six hours, my voice, usually shrill and weak, became full and somewhat sonorous. I could have spoken all night, and I should have done it had the judge attempted to put me down. But I willingly acknowledge that, on the whole, the conduct of the judge was fair to me, and patient to a degree that inspired me with great respect for the dignity of the bench, and I dedicated my 'Short and Easy Method with the Saints' to Mr. Justice Erskine, as an actual expression of my respect. The governor of the gaol one day said to me, that I ought not to regret six months' imprisonment after occupying the court and public so many hours. I did not regret it. Indeed, I more deserved the sentence for the length of my defence than for the words for which I was indicted. But it was the menace of the magistrates (before recounted) that I should not be heard, that did me the harm, and exposed me to the imputation of wanting good sense, which is a worse imputation than that of wanting orthodoxy. This came of inexperience in inprisonment. The menaces of magistrates will not so mislead me another time.

When I now read the notices of these proceedings which I furnished to the *Oracle* at the time, I smile at the juvenility of comment in which I indulged. When similarly-worded reports reach me for the *Reasoner*, my practice is to extract the simple facts—and, of course, the writers remonstrate with me; but how grateful should I be now if some one had done the same by me then. The principle on which we proceeded with our *Oracle* was that every man should express himself in his own words and in his own way, and we thought it a crime against freedom to distinguish between weak comment and the report of essential facts, or the expression of vital principle. The report of the proceedings rendered in these pages is given in some measure upon the rule of discrimination which I have described. But, in this, I have been impartial to others, and have omitted many things on the part of my opponents which I believe they would not repeat, and which I, therefore, have no wish to perpetuate. The remaining variations between this report and that which formerly appeared will be found to be partly on the side of greater accuracy in some respects, and more fulness in others. The original report presented most of the quotations, calling them a string of pearls, but left in a very unravelled state the string which tied them—and hence they read like abrupt interpolations. I have now given the connecting observations, the spirit of the extracts, and, in cases where the extracts have not since that time grown familiar to the public ear, I have given them also.

The influence of my defence upon the public at Gloucester and Cheltenham, notwithstanding the difficulties under which I laboured, was in my favour beyond my expectation. The newspapers stated that 'the court and jury were attentive throughout, and the numbers who thronged the court behaved in the most decorous manner, testifying their interest in the proceedings by a uniform silence, manifesting neither approbation nor disapprobation.' Several newspapers gave nine or ten columns of the proceedings, which was valuable propagandism. And it is due to the *Cheltenham Examiner* (whose parallel between me and Francis the reader will not have forgotten), to state that it gave an effective rendering of my defence, and added these compensatory words to its report :—' The defendant spoke throughout in a temperate manner, and his defence appeared to tell in his favour, so far as regarded the honesty of his motives.'

Let me say here that my grateful acknowledgments are due to the editor of the *Cheltenham Free Press*. That paper reported whatever concerned my liberty, my conscience, or my character. It risked much in defending, alone among its local contemporaries, the freedom of speech violated in my person. It opened its columns to Goodwyn Barmby's proclamations, to Catherine Barmby's letters, to Richard Carlile's defences, and to the numerous communications of my friends on my behalf.

My acknowledgments are also due to the *Weekly Dispatch*. On my visiting London 'Publicola,' then Captain Williams, invited me to call upon him, and inform him of my position with respect to the pending trial ; and his able Letters to Justice Erskine, after my conviction, produced great uneasiness at the gaol, and each number of the *Dispatch* was awaited for some weeks by the authorities around me, as I learned from the gaolers, with anxiety.

My defence, considered as a defence of the wide and momentous question of atheism, was crude enough. No one can be more sensible of that than I am. On the moral aspects of atheism and its relation to public polity I feared to enter, lest in my own newness to the study of so large a subject I should compromise it by unskilfulness of statement ; I therefore confined myself to pleading that the right of public expression was the sequence of the right of private judgment—that the right of expression was consonant to the common law as well as to reason, and that the right of expression being necessary to private morality, it could not be incompatible with the public peace.

CHAPTER III. AFTER THE SENTENCE.

As soon as the sentence was pronounced, I was taken to the cells under the court. Captain Mason, the governor, said there was another prisoner to go down besides me and Adams. It was a case of felony. He said 'Would I go with him?' I replied 'I would not.' He then asked if I 'objected to go with Adams.' That I cheerfully agreed to, and, handcuffed with Adams, I walked down to the gaol. Having taken nothing since morning but a little raspberry vinegar, with which Mr. Carlile supplied me, I began to feel weak, but nothing was offered me except a little warm water, for which I asked, and this, with a very hard and bitter apple, constituted my supper. The transition from the excitement of the court to the darkness and coolness of the night-cell, made me feel as if going into a well, and my supper not serving to compose me, I continued restless till the morning.

Next day I felt so weak that I could scarcely stand upright. About twelve o'clock Mr. Bransby Cooper and the Rev. Samuel Jones came round. When Mr. Cooper saw me, he said, 'Why, Holyoake, I did not know you yesterday.'

'Why, sir?'

'You did not seem to be the same person you were before.'

'In what respect was I different?'

'Before you were so gentle and submissive, but yesterday there was so much *hauteur* about you.'

I answered, 'Here I had to endure your authority; in court I had to defend my character and liberty. It was my turn yesterday, it is yours again to-day.'

About the middle of the first day's imprisonment I was startled by the sonorous voice of the street cryer, passing near the walls of the gaol, crying with a loud voice—' Howitt's correct list of all the cast, quit, and condemned;' and specifying, with marked emphasis, far above that bestowed on two cases of *wilful murder*, the case of 'George Jacob Holyoake, for uttering certain Blasphemous words against God, and of and concerning the Christian Religion.' The above words and specification are to be found in the said ' Correct List,' which a turnkey bought for me at my request, and which I still have. On the second morning after my sentence, I was sitting by the (very little) fire in the common room, contemplating, with very critical air, a can of somewhat indifferent gruel, which I had not the slightest disposition to eat, when the prayer bell rung, which did not at all improve my temper. Where he gaol was situated, I enjoyed such a propinquity to dock bells, basin bells, cathedral bells, and gaol bells, that had I been inclined to re*bel*, it would have chimed in with the others. Upon the aforesaid prayer bell ringing, all my fellow-prisoners made a rapid escape. I could not tell what had become of them. Over my head was a large grating, for the convenience of gaolers overlooking the room. Down this grating there came a tremendous voice, shouting ' Holyoake! Holyoake! Holyoake!' The voice belonged to Ogden, a man whom Carlyle would have delighted to honour. Nature made him for a gaoler. Looking up, I said ' What do you want?'

'Did you not hear that bell?'

'Yes,' I said; 'what of that?'

'All the other prisoners are gone to prayers.'

'Well, let the poor devils go, if they like it.'

'I can't be talked to in this way,' he roared out, in his surliest tones; 'you must go.'

'I am afraid that is a mistake of yours.'

'Don't you know where you are?'

'Yes; I'm in Gloucester Gaol, sitting over a can of very bad gruel.'

'Don't you know you are a prisoner?'

'Oh! yes; I am quite sensible of it.'

'Well, you must do as the others do, and you must go to prayers.'

'Then you must carry me.'

'I'll report you to the clergyman.'

'Give the clergyman my compliments, and say I'm not coming to prayers.'

He stalked away with the air of one whose dignity was greatly outraged. During the time of this colloquy prayers were suspended, and the clergyman was waiting my arrival in order to begin. As soon as prayers were well over, an order came for me —' The clergyman wanted me.'

'Well, Mr. Holyoake,' he said, when I met him, 'how is it you did not come to prayers?'

I answered, 'You cannot expect me to come to prayers; you imprison me here on the ground that I do not believe in a God, and then you would take me to chapel to pray to one. I cannot prevent your imprisoning me, but I can prevent your making me a hypocrite, and must.'

'But if you attended the ordinances of grace, it might lead you to believe in the Christian religion.'

'I should be very sorry for that.'

'Really me—how can you say so, sir?'

'Because I should be very sorry to treat those who differ from me as you treat me.'

'You do not understand us. It is not you we persecute—it is your opinions.'

'Then I wish you would imprison my opinions, and not me.'

Here he turned to refresh himself by looking at the rules for the regulation of prisoners in Gloucester gaol. He resumed—

'But you must attend prayers—it's the rule of the gaol.'

'I must do what I must do, I know; but, if I do that, I must be carried into chapel every morning, and that will not edify the remainder of your congregation. What can I do if I go? I could not say, "O Lord, I have erred and strayed like a lost sheep." You see yonder gratings? I'm not likely to err and stray, for the next six months, beyond those bars.'

'Ah! that is not what we mean.'

'Then what do you mean? Can I join with those men in saying, "O Lord, who hath given us grace with one accord to make our common supplications unto thee," when I shall make no supplications, unless I am forced to it? You know the prisoners only go because the turnkey is behind them?' Then I showed him the passage, 'We have done those things which we ought not to have done,' &c., and asked him what I had done, or had the chance of doing, wrong, since I came there? At this he was puzzled a little, and he at last answered—

'Ah! but we think there is a divine influence in prayer, which might operate upon you.'

'Not in this place,' I answered, 'where it is so much contradicted by your practice. I will agree to this, that when on Sundays you preach, and I may hear something new, I will come.'

He ended the colloquy after a very Christian manner, by saying, 'Well, if you don't come to prayers, you shall be locked up.'

I answered, 'Well, sir, give your orders.' I need scarcely say this was done, in one form or other, to the end of my imprisonment. Sometimes I was locked in my sleeping cell, but generally in the day room; but I found it more agreeable than the litany, and I never asked for any alteration. I went to chapel only on Sunday (the preaching day), but never to the week-day prayers.

Offensive regulations were often sought to be applied to me. One was an attempt to make me wear the prison dress. I said I preferred my own clothes. The answer was, the rules were imperative, and they must enforce them. I inquired whether they had any spare time on their hands, for it would be necessary to dress me every morning. My answer was reported to the magistrates, and I heard no more of the project.

Out of doors much is said against passive resistance, but in prison it is the only resistance possible, and is often very effective. If you speak or act, you are at the mercy of those in whose power you are. Take any aggressive step and your gaoler knocks you down, or locks you up in a moment. But if you simply will not do a thing, if without bluster or bravado you leave it to them to make you do it, or to do it themselves, they often find it of rather awkward accomplishment. To carry me to prayers or to dress me every morning was far more offensive and troublesome to them than breaking my head, so they left me alone.

Old Mr. Jones, the magistrate, paid me frequent visits. One day he took me to the door, and pointing upwards, asked, 'did I not see there proofs sufficient of the existence of a God?' I answered, that 'when the boundless expanse of the skies had been before me I had been unable to think so, and now the few square feet, which the high walls of the gaol permitted me to see, were still less likely to inspire me with that conviction.'

A little reflection ought to have shown these gentlemen, who made these appeals to me, that the time and place were both inauspicious in which to address to me such interrogatories. Indeed it was offensive, and on more than one occasion I told them, that havng undertaken to compel my acquiescence with them by imprisonment, I could never divest myself of the conviction that it was superfluous to pretend to win me by argument.

The last visit Mr. Jones paid was to read me a psalm. As on my trial I had complained of the discourtesy of their calling me a fool, the old man was particularly anxious to justify himself. He found what seemed to him a favourable opportunity in the circumstance that a German scholar had at this time published a new translation of the Psalms of David. As I had spoken favourably of German theologians, he concluded that this one would have weight with me. He brought down the book, summoned the whole class of prisoners, and we stood twelve or eighteen in a row. Proclaiming attention, he said he wished to read to us, and particularly to me, the 14th Psalm. Reading aloud the first verse where David observes 'the fool hath said in his heart there is no God,' Mr. Jones said, 'Now, Holyoake, you complained that we called you a fool—you see David says you are a fool.' The old man looked round with an air of triumph, which was considerably moderated when I gently but distinctly observed that 'I no more liked rudeness in the mouth of David than in the mouth of a magistrate.' My fellow-prisoners glanced around in consternation at my audacity, and expected to hear me ordered into the dark cell, but old Mr. Jones turned round, shut up his book, and walked away without saying a word, and I never saw him afterwards.

The next day I wrote to the Board of Magistrates to say that 'if visiting magistrates continued to question me before other prisoners, where the discipline of the gaol forbade adequate reply,

I should refuse to answer.' In future I was always called out by myself and spoken with alone.

Before my trial the same Mr. Jones told me that my friend, Mr. Richard Carlile, had died in London a very horrible death, recanting all his principles before he expired, and urged me to take warning by his example and do the same. Shortly after Mr. Jones was surprised to meet Mr. Carlile in the corridor of the gaol bringing me refreshments, which his experience assured him I needed. And it was not the least part of my pride on the day of my trial that he sat near me from morning till night, encouraging me by his presence, and assisting me by his wisdom. After my conviction he vindicated me assiduously through the press, addressed to me public letters, and wrote to Justice Erskine and Sir Robert Peel, threatening to renew his former war against the Church if my situation was not ameliorated—a very curious species of recantation it must be confessed, but a fair sample of the usual death-bed 'scenes' which the pulpits relate.

My company as a prisoner was not of a very agreeable kind. I had to listen to recitals of depravity such as I never heard before, and do not wish to hear again. But this was not all. Sometimes a companion was filthy as well as wicked. One man sent in among us had the itch, and before I found it out he had held me by the wrists in some accidental wrestle—which misfortune might have subjected me to a taste of prison discipline which few will be able to imagine.

When the surgeon finds that a prisoner has this disease he makes no remark, but shortly after, the man is called out by the turnkey, whom he has to follow through various corridors to remote cells at the top of the gaol, near the gallows. Upon entering one, he is told to take off his clothes. As soon as he is in a state of nudity, his clothes are taken away, and locked up. He is then shown a cask filled with brimstone, grease, and other mixture, of the consistence of pitch, and quite as offensive to the sight. With this he is made to smear his entire person over; when this is done, he is left locked up in the place. All he finds about him is a bed on which are two blankets, in which hundreds, smeared as he is, have lain before. When no longer able to endure the cold, he may lie in this place. Thick and chilly, these disgusting coverings adjust themselves to the body when softened by the warmth, where, without caution, the liquid will run into the eyes and the mouth. Here he remains some days and eats the uncut food which is brought to him as well as he can with his filthy fingers.

Such is the description of a process of cure (as I gathered from several whose experience I heard narrated), to which I might have been subjected, if, when I discovered pustules on my wrists similar to those on the infected man, I had not kept from the observation of the surgeon while they remained. My habit of daily ablution, and some medicine I procured, saved me from more than temporary discomfort. I need scarcely add, that had such a cure been attempted on me, I should have had to be carried to the place, and the application must have been effected by force.

After some weeks' imprisonment, and when I had had sufficient opportunity of noticing the disposition of the authorities, and estimating the treatment to which I was to be subjected, I addressed the following, slightly abridged—

Memorial of George Jacob Holyoake, prisoner for Blasphemy* in Gloucester County Gaol, to Sir James Graham, her Majesty's Secretary of State.

Sir,—At the recent Gloucester Assizes your memorialist was sentenced by Mr. Justice Erskine to six months' imprisonment for the alleged offence of blasphemy.

Since that period he has been confined in the common gaol and fed on convict gruel, bread, rice, and potatoes. It is true your memorialist is allowed the privilege of purchasing, to some extent, better food, but his imprisonment renders this privilege valueless, without the assistance of friends, upon whom are the claims of his family left dependent by his incarceration.

Under these circumstances your memorialist applied to the surgeon of the gaol for other diet; by the surgeon he was referred to the governor; by the governor to the visiting magistrates, and by the visiting magistrates back to the surgeon, who subsequently has *recommended*, though not prescribed, better diet: but from the recommendation of it, your memorialist concludes that in that gentleman's opinion it is necessary. Two other surgeons whom your memorialist consulted on entering his prison warned him that a generous diet was absolutely requisite, and the decay of your memorialist's health is a testimony of its truth.

He prays for other regulations than those under which he sees VISITORS. They have always to stand, sometimes to talk through the bars of a gate, and are permitted to stay but a few minutes. As your memorialist is far from his friends, these rules continually prevent him seeing them, and receiving those attentions to his wants he otherwise would.

He wishes permission to remain up in an evening until the hour of the debtors' retiring (9 o'clock), or at least to be allowed the use of a light in his cell, in which he is confined from twelve to fourteen hours, and during the winter he will be so shut up sixteen hours and a half. Thus much time will be lost your memorialist could employ upon a little mathematical speculation,† which would afford him the gratification of contributing himself to the support of his family.

As every *newspaper* sent your memorialist is retained by the governor, your memorialist prays the liberty of reading them.

The visiting magistrates have said they should have no objection to grant what your memorialist asks, had they the power; and hence he prays the exercise of your authority on his behalf.

---

* I always said 'Prisoner for Blasphemy' in all my communications, and directed my friends so to address me, to which the magistrates objected. But if I was to be written to at a gaol, I preferred to be known as a prisoner for opinion rather than as a prisoner for crime.

† Mentioned to prevent the supposition on the part of Sir James that the time would be employed in writing blasphemy, which would be fatal to the application.

As custom attaches little weight to the opinion of a prisoner, it becomes not your memorialist to speak of his own case, but trusts he may with propriety refer to it as one in which he believes will be found little that is aggravated. Seduced in the warmth of debate to express his honest opinion on a religious question, young and inexperienced, he took not the hypocrite's crooked path, nor the dissembler's hidden way, but unwarily uttered language disingenuousness would have concealed or art have polished, and became in consequence the ready victim of Christianity. Criminal without intention, punishment brings with it no consciousness of guilt, and hence that which in other circumstances would be light, is, in his, a bitter infliction.

GEORGE JACOB HOLYOAKE.

Sir James gave me permission to remain up till 9 o'clock after I had been three months in prison. But for the concession it required an effort to be grateful, for it was a permission to remain up without fire and without light. For unless I could pay for fire and light, I had to go without. Whether Sir James Graham intended this, I have no means of knowing; he probably expected that the magistrates would not interpret his order as a privilege to sit up in the cold and in the dark, which would be a greater punishment than going to bed. But they did put this construction upon it. As Sir James did not mention fire and light, they refused to supply them.

Mathematical studies were impossible, for the authorities also refused to allow me my instruments, lest I should commit suicide with them; but I had provided for that, as every man should who goes to gaol. There was just width enough in my cell to admit of the heavy iron bed-frame being raised on one end. By marking a circle round one of the legs, which I did with a fragment of stone, I determined the place on which the leg would fall when the frame was pulled down. My head once placed on that spot, the great weight of the frame would have sent the narrow leg through the brain, and death must have been instantaneous. I am no friend of suicide, and had a thousand reasons for living; but I had not been long in gaol before I saw many things to which none but the degraded or the weak would submit—and lest they should come to my turn, I provided against them.

About this time an event occurred in my family which converted my imprisonment into an unexpected bitterness. Against that 'love abroad which means spite (or indifference) at home,' I early set my face. Between me and Eleanor, my wife, there always existed an understanding as to the risks I ran in my free speaking. Whatever consequences fell upon my own head alone, I had myself only to please in incurring: but those which affected others, I had no right to invoke, without their consent—and this consent I always sought from my wife, in any special case which arose. At our marriage, Eleanor very well understood that my life somewhat resembled a soldier's, and that it would often include duties and dangers not compatible with perennial fireside comfort. Nor did she object to this, and I have had the sweet fortune always to be left to do whatever I should have done, had I been single and childless. On my saying, on the imprisonment of Mr. Southwell, first editor of the *Oracle*, that it was my duty to take his place, Eleanor replied—' Do what it seems your duty to do, and I and the children will take care of ourselves as well as we can. When they grow up, I trust they will contemplate with little satisfaction any advantage they might have enjoyed at the expense of their father's duty. We can leave them no riches, but we may at least leave them a good example, and an unsoiled name.'

It was therefore that when I came to leave home, to go to my Trial, all was calm and cheerful as usual, though there was much around to suggest uneven thoughts. On that day no one came to accompany me or to spend an hour of solace with those from whom I parted. Had there been a single friend present to have made up the appearance of society after I was gone, the loneliness would have been less bitter. As I left the house I heard that cry break forth which had been suppressed that it might not sadden my departure. Before I had proceeded far up Windsor Street, Ashted, I was arrested by Madeline's silvery voice calling ' good bye, dada,' and turning round I saw her large bright, black eyes (which every body praised) peering like two stars round the lintel of the door. I am glad I did not then know that I should never hear that voice again, nor see those bright eyes any more.

To turn the attention of mankind in an atheistical direction may do harm to some. The propagation of all new views does harm, more or less. As in commercial speculations much capital is sunk before any returns come in, so in the improvement of the people, you sacrifice some old feeling which is good, before the new opinion, which is better, can be created. But all the new opinions I have at any time imbibed have never produced so much harm in me as the prudential doctrines of Political Economy. The doctrine that it is disreputable in the poor to have children, is salutary, no doubt—but it requires to be enforced under limitation. To regard the existence of your little ones as an expense, and the gentle love of children as a luxury in which you cannot indulge without reproach, is to sour life, dry up affection, and blight those whose tender years should be passed in a perpetual smile of joy. To look into the face of your child and feel that the hand of death, which shall hush that gentle voice, pale those rosy cheeks, and quench those animated eyes—is a political blessing, is horrible. I look back with mute terror on the days when I was under the influence of those feelings. I cannot dwell upon it. I would burn all the books of Political Economy I ever read (and I think it the science of many blessings) if I could feel once more on my knee the gentle hand of my child from whom I parted that day, too stoical to shed a tear.

After a few weeks of my imprisonment had passed away, hint-words came of Madeline's failing health. Out of some money sent by my private friends, John Fowler and Paul Rodgers, of Sheffield, to buy better food than the gaol afforded, I saved a guinea and sent it to Birmingham to purchase Madeline a winter cloak—it was spent in buying her a coffin. Though of perfect health and agility, she was one of those children who require entire preservation from exposure, want, or fatigue. On ten shillings per week, which was all that the Anti-Persecution Union could provide, this could not be done, as Eveline, then in arms, left her mother no opportunity of increasing that small income. Cold succeeded cold, when want of more means caused them all to go to live in a house ill ventilated, and where several were ill of fever, which soon attacked Madeline.

Mr. Chilton sent me several intimations to prepare for the worst, should it happen. But I could not believe in the worst happening, and indeed I had yet to realise what the worst implied. At length one morning the heavy corridor door grated on its harsh hinges, and the morose turnkey — fit messenger of misery—put a letter into my hand. As it had been, as usual, broken open—for there is no feeling, not even that of affection and death, respected in a gaol—Ogden knew its contents, and in justice to him I must say he endeavoured, as well as one whose ability lay in his moroseness could, to speak a word of apology and sympathy. The strangeness and awkwardness of the attempt drew my attention to the fatal black border, which gave me sensations such as I never received before and never shall again, for the first death of one dear to you, like that of the first love, brings with it a feeling which is never repeated. I remember that some prisoner came and covered me with a coat, for I had walked into the yard without one. Captain Mason and two friends came round, but I could not speak to them. He addressed a few words to me, but I turned away.

Then Madeline had died the death of the poor; she had perished among the people who know neither hope nor comfort, a pledge that I shall never forsake those with whose sad destiny one so dear to me is linked. Though in the death of poverty there is nothing remarkable, though hundreds of children are daily killed off in the same way, yet parents unused to this form of calamity find in it, the first time, a bitterness which can never be told. The ten shillings per week income of the family was made up by small subscriptions by some who knew me, and by a few outside who happened to think useful the course I had taken. One or two friends whose professions had beforetime been profuse, Eleanor met. They were cold, or to her they seemed so. She thought they feared a continued acquaintance might lay them under some tax to contribute to her support. This she could never bear. Offering her hand to one who did not take it, she went home, and nothing induced her to subject herself to such suspicion any more. A quick and enduring sense of independence, which no privation could disturb, was an attribute in her character I had always admired, and this dreadful form of its operation I have never been able to censure. The Roman mother put on the armour of her son as he went out, and saw him brought home dead from the fight without weakness: but in that case, the strife of arms, the glory of victory, the sublimity of duty, and the applause of the senate, were so many supports to the mother's heroism; but harder far is it for a mother to bend over her child day by day and night after night, and see relentless death eat like a canker into the bud of the damask cheek of beauty, and be too poor to snatch it from the tomb—and this with no trumpet note, no clang of arms to drown the dying scream, no incense of glory to raise the sinking heart, no applause of a generous people to reward the sacrifice—without one soul near who could penetrate to the depth of that desolation, and utter those words of sympathy which is all which humanity can do to soothe in the face of death. There were indeed those near who might have done so, but some could not comprehend this grief, and others, for reasons of Political Economy, 'did not see the good of regret' at a child dying, and they will learn from these pages for the first time that these wounds existed which, after eight years, are still fresh.

> There are homesteads that have witnessed deeds
> That battle fields, with all their bannered pomp,
> Have little to compare with. Life's great play
> May, so it have an *actor* great enough,
> Be well performed upon a humble stage.

'My dada's coming to see me,' Madeline exclaimed on the night of her death, with that full, pure, and thrilling tone which marked her when in health. ' I am sure he is coming to night, mama,' and then remembering that that could not be, she said 'write to him, mama, he will come to see me;' and these were the last words she uttered—and all that remains now is the memory of that cheerless, fireless room, and the midnight reverberation of that voice which I would give a new world to hear again.

For her father, he was debating in incoherence the vain proposition as to whether he could prevail on the Governor to let him go home for one night to smooth and watch over that dying pillow, and he would cheerfully and gratefully have expiated the privilege by six or twelve months' additional imprisonment.

O Liberty! whom the nations welcome with triumphant shouts, whom all to whom the world owes its progress have worshipped —over how many graves hast thou walked! Rising with the morning's dawn, making all people radiant with thy presence, the poet thrills as thy chariot is borne on the sun's golden beams, and he hails thee as a goddess, and blesses thee as a bride, and sings of thy triumphs and benefactions! But those who serve thee—who make their lives a sad and desert waste that thy pathway through the world may be unobstructed—who kneel to thee in their dungeon-churches and pour out the incense of life's young warm blood at gibbet-altars: *they* know thee by thy gory garments dripping with the blood of the father and the tear of the orphan, and the desolation which precedes thy progress. The anthems of thy march are hollow voices from Siberia's mines, and Vincennes' cells—the wail of women under the Russian knout, the groans of Konarski and the whistle of bullets which slay the Bandiera and Blum—thy trophies are the fresh graves of Hungary and Rome, thy throne is on a hecatomb of earth's noblest and bravest sons. Yet art thou still sacred in the eyes of man. Queen of Genius and Progress! emblem of that suffering through which Humanity is purified and developed! Thou hast trodden on the grave of my child, and I worship thee still, although thou mayst yet tread on my own.

Yes, though I neither hope—for that would be presumptuous— nor expect it, seeing no foundation, I shall be pleased to find a life after this. Not a life where those are punished who were unable to believe without evidence, and unwilling to act in spite of reason—for the prospect of annihilation is pleasanter and more profitable to contemplate: not a life where an easy faith is regarded as 'easy virtue' is regarded among some men—but a life where those we have loved and lost here are restored to us again—for there, in that Hall where those may meet who have been sacrificed in the cause of duty—where no gross, or blind, or selfish, or cruel nature mingles, where none sit but those whom human service and endurance have purified and entitled to that high company, Madeline will be a Hebe. Yes, a future life, bringing with it the admission to such companionship, would be a noble joy to contemplate. But Christianity has no such dream as this.

On making arrangements for the burial, at the Birmingham Cemetery, the clerk asked whether they should provide a Minister, or whether the friends of the deceased would do so? The answer was—'A minister was not desired.' Then I presume,' the clerk observed, 'you mean that you will provide one yourselves?' The answer again was, 'we do not require one at all. Please send the beadle merely.'

On the day of the interment the beadle attended as requested.

He was instructed to conduct the burial party direct to the grave, and not into the chapel, which he did without remark: and when the coffin, plain but pretty, without tinsel or angels, was lowered, each threw a bouquet of flowers in, and when the grave was made up they returned home. Thus Madeline was buried, as became her innocence and her fate, without parade, without priest, or priestly ceremony. Had hesitation been displayed, or previous inquiries been made as to whether what was done could have been permitted, no question but that a priest would have been inflicted, as at the grave of Carlile and others—for Christianity, always officious and rude to the dissentient, is never more so than when opposition is paralysed by agony on the bed of death, or hushed in speechless sadness by the side of the grave.

As it would only be painful to Mrs. Holyoake, I never wished her to visit me; but after the death of Madeline she desired it, and she brought little 'Eveline' (a name given to her in lieu of her own because of its similarity to Madeline.) On this occasion Mr. Bransby Cooper sent to say that the magistrates' Committee-room, an elegant and cheerful apartment, should be at my service, at Mrs. Holyoake's visit. Mr. Cooper was the first of the magistrates to send a message of condolence on the death of Madeline, and in this instance his kindness was delicate and generous. As on the day Mrs. Holyoake came the magistrates happened to hold a meeting in it, an apology was sent me, and the Lodge placed at my service. No turnkey was sent in, and I was permitted to see my friends with an air of perfect freedom. My sister Caroline, who was one of the party, brought me a present of wine and cigars. As both were forbidden by the rules of the gaol, I declined to touch them. As I was trusted without restraint, I was doubly anxious to respect a liberty so generously conceded. Had they set a watch over me, I should have had less scruple, and perhaps have thought it a merit to defeat their suspicions.

Captain Mason, the governor, was a study — a type of the gentleman, official, and conventional, whose qualities were instructive. Bland, imperturbable, civil, and firm, he was never weak and never rude. Among the uneducated, all decisive action is announced in commotion or bluster. The gentleman is never in a hurry, never in a contention. If you annoy him, are rude to him, impose upon him, or menace him, perhaps he quietly indicates his opinion of the impropriety, perhaps his resolution is taken without. He avoids you. His defence is prevention. Renewal of offence, renewal of intercourse, chance of altercation or repetition, is simply impossible. Such was Captain Mason. I watched his manners with pleasure—he governed the gaol like a drawing room, excepting that the *desserts* were not quite the same. I saw rude men baffled, they could not make out how. Possibly he had nerves and sensibility, but these articles were not in common use. They were kept under lock and key, and never brought out in the routine of official duties. As blandly and courteously as he wished me good morning, he would have conducted me to the gallows, had instruction to that effect reached him. He would have apologised for the inconvenience, but he would have hung me while I was saying 'pray don't mention it.'

Excepting in one transaction our intercourse was unruffled. When I had left the gaol, a prisoner (the Master of a Post Office) the only gentleman on my side of the prison, addressed to me a letter of accusation against the governor—an act which made me a participator in his sentiments. As it passed through the governor's hands, he wrote under the name the crime and sentence of the writer—a brief and bitter retort. I re enclosed the letter to the writer with a note to Captain Mason, observing that on leaving the gaol I had expressed to him the only opinion I entertained of him, and I should regard it as unmanly to be a party to reproaches which I did not see reason to address to him in person. He wrote me back, with a soldier's honourable frankness, that 'I had always behaved honourably in my intercourse with him, and he did not believe I would do an unmanly thing.'

The exceptional transaction with the Captain referred to was this. One of my fellow-prisoners was an epileptic man, whose ignorance and irritability, more than any crime, had led to his imprisonment. As I kept a sort of school in our common room, and taught a few things to those about me who were disposed to learn, I had become interested in Upton, a humble and unhappy man, who learned *at* grammar anxiously. Some nights he would fall out of bed in an epileptic fit, and lie groaning on the stone floor for an hour or more together. It was in vain that we shouted to the turnkeys. They who can hear a man *think* of escaping, cannot hear when he breaks his neck. Upton representing that a little tobacco, to which he had been accustomed, would save him from the frequency of these fits, I procured him some. Smoking it one day in a corner, in a paper pipe made for the purpose out of one of my letters, the governor came upon him through a side door. Upon being asked how he procured it, he answered, 'From a man who had just come in from the Sessions.' This the governor did not believe. At night Ogden made an immense speech at me, in which that luminous functionary inserted several elephantine hints, to the effect that he knew the source whence the aforesaid tobacco came. It was a treat to hear Ogden hint; it was like a hippopotamus putting his paw out, or kicking a man down stairs. As soon as I could get to speak to Upton, I prevailed upon him to allow me to write to the governor, tell him the truth, and take the blame upon myself, reminding Upton that a good man might be surprised into a lie, but only a bad man would persist in one. The retaliation of the governor was refined and vindictive. Instead of ordering me into a dark cell on bread and water for two or three days, which was the authorised punishment, he ordered two gates to be locked between me and my visitors, so that those who spoke were obliged to shout to me. This he continued, with slight variation, to the end of my imprisonment. This deprived me of the pleasure of seeing ladies who called, as I would never consent to see them under circumstances of so much humiliation.

Captain Mason had had previous proof that my professions might be trusted. When first imprisoned, the reader perhaps remembers I was kept (though on my way home after a journey) a fortnight while the magistrates played at bail. When at length they signified their intention of accepting it, Captain Mason took me, through the city, to Bransby Cooper's house, where the bail-deed was to be completed. On our way I asked him if it would be necessary for me to take an oath, before my own bond could be accepted, as I should object to take an oath? He turned round and replied—'Why, Holyoake, as you don't believe in any of the Gods, you could have no objection to swear by them all.' I explained to him that if the Magistrate would regard my oath as a mere ceremony, by which I rendered myself liable to penalties in case of violated truth or failure in my bond, I would take the oath readily, if all the Gods of the Pantheon were in it: but if it were regarded as a profession of my religious faith, I would not take it. It was better that I should go back to gaol, than to make a profession of belief which would mislead others. I told Mr. Cooper the same when we reached his house. He, however, said my signature would do.

One day I concluded a dialogue with my chaplain upon the principle of reciprocation, *i. e.*, of retorting his language upon himself, and, I think, not without utility, for he never afterwards fell into that insensible arrogance of speech so common among pastors. On the occasion referred to, he began—

'Are you really an atheist, Mr. Holyoake?'

'Really I am.'

'You deny that there is a God?'

'No; I deny that there is sufficient reason to believe that there is one.'

'I am very glad to find that you have not the temerity to say that there is no God.'

'And I am very sorry to find that you have the temerity to say there is one. If it be absurd in me to deny what I cannot demonstrate, is it not improper for you to assert so dogmatically what you cannot prove?'

'Then where would you leave the question of atheism?'

'Just where it leaves us both. It is a question of probability.'

'Ah! the probabilities in favour of atheism are very few.'

'How know you that? Did you ever examine the question without prejudice, or read that written in its favour without fear? Those who dare not look at all never see far.'

'But if the atheist has so much on his side, why does he not make it known? *We* do not keep back *our* evidences.'

'Has the atheist an equal opportunity with you? Is it generous in you to taunt him with lack of evidence, when you are prepared to punish its production?'

'The reason is that your principles are so horrible; as Robert Hall has said, 'Atheism is a bloody and ferocious system.''

'Permit me, sir, to return that gentle speech—to tell you that your principles are horrible, and that Christianity is a bloody and ferocious system.'

'Really I am shocked to hear you speak so dreadfully of Christianity.'

'Why should you be shocked to hear what you are not shocked to say?'

'But atheism is so revolting.'

'But Christianity is so revolting.'

'How dangerous is it for atheism to corrupt the minds of children.'

'How pernicious is it for Christian doctrines to corrupt the thoughts of infancy.'

'But you are only asserting.'

'Are you doing otherwise? I sometimes think that Christians would be more respectful in their speech if the same language could be applied to them with impunity which they apply to others.'

'But, my dear sir, the language of the atheist is so shocking to Christian feeling.'

'And, my dear sir, has it never occurred to you that the language of the Christian is shocking to atheistical feeling?'

'Atheists have a right to their opinions, I allow, but not to publish them.'

'I shall think you speak reasonably when you permit the same rule to be applied to the Christian.'

'But you really cannot be an atheist?'

'And you say this who have been a party to imprisoning me here for being one! If you believe yourself, go and demand my liberation.'

'Ah! when you come to die you will wish that you were a Christian.'

'Can it be that I shall wish to hold a creed that I distrust—one that leads me to deny another the liberty I claim for myself? If to be capable of looking back with satisfaction on conduct like this is to be a Christian, may I never die the death of the righteous, and may my last end never be like his.'

As the general treatment pursued towards me did not work an satisfactory conversion, some attempts were made by gentler means. Taken one day into a sleeping cell for privacy, one who had the power to fulfil his promises passed in review the casualties of a life like mine, and asked whether I had not better change it. Thinking I was seduced by some attraction which belonged to my position, he suggested how fickle a thing was popularity, and how soon the applause of friends might die away, or change with the growth or refinement of my conviction, into suspicion or even hate. Had I not better accept the editorship of a paper, where I should not be required to contradict, but merely to avoid advocating my views? Had I not better accept a school in a retired part of the country—a girls' school also might be given to Mrs. Holyoake, and our joint incomes would ensure competence, respectability, and usefulness? I answered, 'I think you have mistaken me. The opinions I defended are also my convictions; and thinking them useful, it seems my duty to propagate them, and the discharge of this duty is more serious in my eyes than you suppose; nor do the inducements you picture exist. Do you not see that I am nearly friendless? I am without even the attentions of those from whom I have some right to expect it. Except Mr. Farn, Mr. Watts, and Mr. Campbell, none of my colleagues among the Social Missionaries have written me a friendly word. The editor of the *New Moral World*, upon whose protection I have some claim, has written no word in my favour. The only public defence for which I am indebted has come from strange papers, and unknown men. Even Mr. Owen, the advocacy of whose opinions involved me in this prosecution, he who occupied the largest share of my veneration, has not even recognised my existence by a single line. This affair may have made some noise, but I am not so young as to mistake noise for popularity, nor so weak as to think popularity the one thing needful. Popularity is to be won by those who can flatter the public, but that estimation which is alone worth having is only to be won by the service of the people, and that is not the work of youth but of life. That which you call my cause is yet in an infantine state. It has no attractions but the rude ones of daring and truth. It requires to be divested of antagonism, and developed in its relations to political and social interests and personal character. This must be the work of time, and judging from the present, it will be a work of difficult and precarious effort. At present we number no public friends of wealth or influence. We have every thing to gain—yet the comparative affluence you offer would be a canker to my peace, while it was the price of duty evaded. My self-chosen path, presumptuous and thorny, will be sweeter to walk. It is enough that you see I am not misled by its attractions. Now I tread these floors with a proud step, and meet your eye with unblenched brow, because it is necessary to show you that in defence of my opinions I feel neither fear nor guilt—but when I walk from this place into the wilderness of the world, my steps will falter and my face will pale, because my path will lie over the grave of my child.'

All I remember farther is that my tempter made a few not unfeeling remarks, and led me back in silence to my usual cell.

The final efforts for my conversion were on this wise. The Rev. Mr. Cooper sent for me, a few days before my liberation, and asked me to follow him to the chapel. Arrived there, he ascended the pulpit, motioning me to a prisoner's pew without even asking me to be seated. My neck was stiff with a severe cold, and I was as ill able as ill disposed to be catechised. I stood leaning on the spikes—not inapt emblems of such Christian love as I had there been made acquainted with. The good Chaplain prayed—I did not move. He looked at me to catch my eye—I kept mine fixed on the spikes. He addressed me—I made no sign. He spoke some minutes—still I remained motionless. He paused and asked what I thought of his representations—I answered no word. He seemed to think he was making a favourable impression. He resumed, and came to another peroration, and again besought me to answer—still no motion, no word from me. He began a third time, and touched all serious topics which he could command, and came again to an elaborate peroration on death-beds; and as I remained still silent and immovable, he said, somewhat perplexed this time, 'Holyoake, won't you speak?' I then answered 'Not while we occupy these places. Do you not preach to me and place me here where prisoners stand ? I take this to be a ceremony, and not a conversation.' He walked down from his pulpit and asked me to accompany him, when he took me into several cells till he found one warmed with hot air, and asked would I speak with him there on friendly terms? I answered, 'with pleasure;' and there we conversed for the last time. I troubled him to repeat his arguments, as I would not admit that I had attended to a word. When he had done, I briefly assured him that my experience there had not created in me any desire to be a Christian : he had brought before me no new evidences, and as it had been found necessary to enforce those I knew before by penal reasons, the operation had rather diminished their weight in my estimation.

He professed himself anxious to 'present me with a Bible'—a fact which I knew was destined to make a figure in the next Gaol Report to the County Magistrates; I therefore resolved to have one worth acceptance, or not one at all. When he brought to me the usual prison copy, I respectfully declined it. I said, a thin copy bound in calf, in pearl type, with marginal references, would be interesting to me, but the dumpling-shaped book he offered, I could never endure in my library. He deliberated—the trade price of the Bible he offered me was about tenpence, that I desiderated would cost him half a guinea. The reflection was fatal. The Bible never came, and the evangelical fact that 'The prisoner George Jacob Holyoake was presented with a copy of the Holy Scriptures before leaving the gaol, which it is hoped, under the Divine blessing, will be the means of bringing him to the knowledge of the truth'—was never recorded.

About this period I saw the magistrates for the last time. There seemed to be a full Board of them, and Mr. Bransby Cooper was in the chair. Before withdrawing I addressed Mr. Cooper, and said—' As in a short time I shall leave this place, I wish, before doing so, to express to you my sense of the kindness and consideration shown me by you when Mrs. Holyoake visited me here. It is one of the few things I shall remember with pleasure when again at liberty. You will not, I fear, believe in the possibility of one of my opinions feeling gratitude, but I will at least assure you of it.' The answer he made was a compensation for much that I had experienced. In that loud voice in which he usually spoke, he exclaimed—' Yes, I will say this, that I believe you, Holyoake. I don't believe that you could be a hypocrite.'

One day a magistrate, described to me as the Hon. and Rev. Andrew Sayer, sent me a copy of Paley's works, requesting my particular attention to his Natural Theology. 'Did I put into your hands,' I said, addressing that gentleman, 'an atheistic work, you would tell me of the contamination you dread; and may I not plead the same risk in perusing your theistical book? But, as all in the search after truth must venture through phases of error, I shall not hesitate to comply with your request; and that you may be certain that I do so, you may, when I have ended, put to me any question upon the contents you please.' It happened that my examination resulted in my writing 'Paley Refuted in his Own Words.' When Mr. Sayer came to ask me what conclusions I had come to on the books he had lent me, I made this answer to him—' Sir, I am surprised at your asking me this question. Does it become you, a clergyman and a magistrate, to ask me to commit crime?'

'What do you mean?' he inquired.

'I mean this,' I replied, 'that in having punished my last

expression of opinion as a crime, by bringing me here, it does not become you to put religious inquiries to me again.' He seemed confounded; and on this occasion I showed him, that while Christianity punished as crime the expression of dissentient opinions, Christians were disqualified from seeking the state of any man's thoughts with respect to religion. Unless one volunteers explanations, Christians have plainly no right to demand them. They put themselves out of the pale of ordinary privilege.

Writing 'Paley Refuted' and the 'Short and Easy Method with the Saints'—a title suggested by 'Leslie's Short and Easy Method with the Deists,' another book put into my hands by the authorities—occupied me till the end of my imprisonment. On the 6th of February, 1843, I was liberated; and three days after (having paid visits of acknowledgment to my friends in Gloucester, Cheltenham, and Worcester) I rejoined (what I might then term the remains of) my family in Birmingham.

CHAPTER IV. AFTER THE LIBERATION.

On rejoining my colleagues of the *Oracle of Reason*, I proceeded to issue an address to our readers. The substance of it, which was as follows, comprises some additional facts of my prison experience:—

'MY FRIENDS,—It is now six months since cut and hacked, "I fell," not merely in the language of the parable but literally, "among thieves." Of those who caused that contact, I am afraid I must say, as William Hutton said of an untoward sweetheart— "There was little love between us at first, and heaven has been pleased to decrease it on a further acquaintance." Christians profess to draw men to Jesus with "cords of love," but were it not for their judicious foresight in telling us that they are "cords of love," few would find it out.

'To friends in Gloucester,*Cheltenham, Birmingham, London,†

---

* To Gloucester two special acknowledgments are due. First to a young lady, the niece of the Innkeeper, in whose house I resided, when awaiting Trial, both at the sessions and assizes. With no other knowledge of me than these occasions afforded, and with no prepossession in favour of my opinions, but simply from that generous sympathy women often display, she frequently brought me refreshments to the gaol, and was a medium of communication with my friends, and often answered inquiries of my family which the restrictions of the gaol sometimes rendered it impossible for me even to know. In the romance of incident, she afterwards became the wife of my friend Mr. Chilton. The other instance was that of Mrs. Price, a woman in humble circumstances, who, during the latter part of my imprisonment, brought me dinner every Sunday. Both Mrs. Price and her husband were utterly unknown to me.

† At the time of the death of Madeline, Mrs. Ralph Thomas, of London, sent to Mrs. Holyoake £3, subscribed by herself and personal friends.

and other places, I owe many thanks for what has been contributed for my support, and for that of my family, during my imprisonment. For their attentions I believe no thanks were asked and none are wished. Yet I am concerned to make acknowledgments, because a man always values highly the kindness he does not expect. When the words were spoken which led to my prosecution, I expected that the cautious would think that I had gone "too far"—that the prudent would think that I had been too rash—that my friends would be afraid for me, and that the timid would be afraid for themselves. But I held with Polydamus, that

> To speak his thoughts is every freeman's right—
> In peace and war, in council and in fight.

'And, what I regarded as greater than my right, I felt it to be my duty. Besides, my honour was concerned. I could not descend to that disingenuousness I had often counselled others to scorn. Hence, in the course I took, I did not think it necessary to calculate consequences; a man's true concern is with his principles, and not with his fate. I pretended to no public virtue, and I laid claim to no praise—I did no more than every man ought to do. That doing so little has been so rewarded by the exertions of many friends for my protection, I must be pleased—but had nothing been done, I trust I should have found pride in penury and satisfaction under neglect, in the reflection that I had discharged my duty and preserved consistency.

'When my memorial to Sir James Graham was returned to the magistrates for their opinion, they came to me, and Mr. Bransby Cooper stormed out with great violence—" You were sent here, sir, for punishment, and you have nothing else to expect. I consider you worse than the greatest felon in the gaol; you have been guilty of the most atrocious crime a man can possibly commit. I have told Sir James Graham what you deserve." I knew that these magistrates were Christians. I was told they were gentlemen, but I thought them furies.*

'The prison diet was bread, gruel, and potatoes. On two days in each week boiled rice was substituted for potatoes; and after I had been in prison nine weeks I was, by the rules, allowed a small portion of salt beef on Thursdays and Sundays. As this fare is deemed in Gloucestershire a famous specific for the cure of atheism, it may not be out of place to explain its virtues. The

---

* Yet such is the inconsistency of the Christian character when allied to a generous nature, that Mr. Bransby Cooper who, as a Christian, behaved with so much rudeness, had just before given instruction to the turnkeys to treat me with respect, with a view to save me from less harshness from other officials than that which, in other moods, *he* so plentifully inflicted on me himself.

gruel was little remarkable for its delicate flavour and little celebrated for its nutritious qualities, and known by the luxurious cognomen of " skilly." The rice had a blue cast, a saline taste, and a slimy look. The beef I could not often taste, seldom chew, and never digest—I should say it was rather *leather* mode than *à la mode*. The whole of the food could only be taken by a ploughman's appetite, and only be digested by a navigator's stomach.

'The indirect occasion of my prosecution was the editorship of the *Oracle*. When Mr. Southwell was apprehended no Social Missionary came forward to continue his paper, although many of them were better qualified to do so than myself. Socialism had always attached great importance to freedom of expression, and Socialism's advocates had been styled "apostles of freethought." Knowing this, I felt that it would be a dishonourable reflection should any one refuse personally to support what he was known publicly to approve. Had Mr. Fleming been placed in Mr. Southwell's situation, and had he been of opinion that I could have defended his violated liberty by taking his place, I should have edited the *New Moral World* as cheerfully as I did the *Oracle of Reason*. When I speak of "freedom of speech" and "liberty for all," I know of no distinction between myself and those who differ from me—I see with an equal eye the Atheist and the Christian, the violent and the gentle, the dogmatic and the modest.

'That is true of Christianity which has been said of Catholicism, "Humane individuals may express their abhorrence of the sentiments of persecution—bodies of men, sections of the church itself, nay many of the dignitaries may abjure them, and protest that they have never acted upon them, nor ever will enforce them—yet all this will not avail to give a discerning man the smallest security for his liberty, his property, or his life; for as long as those intolerant decrees remain upon the statute book, they can at any time be revived." It therefore behoves every one to set a guard over that liberty, for the loss of which no religion will ever compensate. The conviction should be permanent that Christianity is a fearful thing. But bad men may laud it—mistaken men may contend that there is some good in it—unthinking men may give currency to its terms—and weak men may connive at its delusions, but we ought to regard with different sentiments a system which tramples upon the feelings of humanity and the principles of liberty. Let us then secure the antidote—free expression of opposite opinion. Shall it be said that we are content to wear mental fetters? When Protestants, who dare never think without the Bible and Prayer Book, have shaken off the iron despotism of Catholicism—when Methodists and even

Ranters have refused to submit their thoughts to be cut down to the Procrustean bed of conventional opinion—let not Christians mock at Freethinking pusillanimity and deride us as holders of craven principles. Not only for ourselves but for others are our exertions demanded. What patrimony has the poor man but his free thoughts? Industry will not save him from chill penury's grip, nor virtue from the poor-house grave—let us then preserve and perfect the humble inheritance of those who have no other.'*

In prison it is not *safe* to make complaints. You are too much in the power of those around you to escape reprisals of a serious kind, but this did not deter me from what I conceived to be a duty, and which might make the future easier for others who might follow me in the same way. Besides the endeavours I had made within the prison, with a view to tolerable treatment, I addressed, on my release, the following letter to the editor of the *Cheltenham Free Press*:—

'MR. EDITOR,—As prisons and prison discipline have lately occupied much public attention, I am induced to offer to your notice a little recent experience in such matters. What I have written, I intended to have stated to a public meeting, but suffering from debility, which makes me glad to avoid excitement, I seek the calmer medium of your paper.

' I speak of Gloucester County Gaol. I believe the prison inspector is of opinion that the rules of that place are "*harsh* and *cruel.*" Now, should a prisoner seek a partial exemption from their operation, the process he goes through is very curious. He applies to a turnkey—the turnkey answers, "my duty is determinate and my province clear; I cannot do it." Probably, he refers the prisoner to the surgeon. The surgeon is seen—he refers him to the governor, the governor refers him to the visiting magistrates—they reply, " we have no power to grant the request, Sir James Graham only can do that." Sir James Graham is memorialised, who, as is usual, answers, " The visiting magistrates best know what is proper—I only grant what they recommend." Any further application to them would be construed into a wilful annoyance, and the prisoner is fortunate who can sit down like Sterne's happy man—pleased he knows not *why*, and contented he knows not *wherefore*. Of course I blame no one, for there is no one to blame, and this constitutes the beauty of the system.†

---

* Revised and abridged from the *Oracle*.

† It seemed to me useful to make applications for what I wanted in writing. It prevented mistakes, and afterwards admitted of proof. The governor used to come to me and say, ' Now, Holyoake, it is of no use sending this memorial. It is sure not to be attended to,' and he would so obligingly bestow upon me the treasures of his experience on the futility of the course I was

Should I individualise, it would only be to say, that the governor is a gentleman of some excellent qualities, and some unintelligible conduct; that the surgeon possesses the *suaviter in modo* WITHOUT the *fortiter in re;* and that the magistrates are little gods, who, like Jupiter, thunder oftener than they smile.

'What of health I have, I owe to my friends, who supplied me with such food as my constitution required, for had I been compelled to subsist on the diet of the prison, my health, by this time, would have been quite broken. With the direction of my own medical adviser, I made this representation to the proper authorities at the gaol; I made them to the commissioners who were lately there, and I made them to Sir James Graham;* I therefore conceive that I am justified in repeating them here. The surgeon *admitted* the necessity of better diet, but referred me to the governor, and he sent me the fruitless round I have described. Now the province of the governor was the care of my person, and the province of the surgeon the care of my health. The governor ought not to have *permitted* the reference to him, and the surgeon ought not to have made it. Either the surgeon should have refused my application with decision, or have allowed it with independence. Upon this subject, the commissioners reminded me, "that if the surgeon did not order what was necessary for my health, he was responsible for it." I replied "that I knew this, and that they also knew, that a prisoner, like Beale of Northleach, must die before he could avail himself of such responsibility, and that this was but *grave* consolation. But of the

pursuing, that at times it really did seem not only useless but uncivil to persist. But I used to say, 'Captain Mason, I suppose you are right as to the result. That makes no difference, however, as to my duty; you may put my memorials in the fire, if you like, as soon as I have written them; still I will make the proper application to every officer and every authority, and deliver them to your care, as in duty bound.' I knew the Captain would not burn them—I knew more, I knew he dare not burn them. I knew, also, that each would be duly delivered to the proper party. Further I knew this, that if his dissuasions had deterred me from sending in my complaints, that when I left the prison the authorities would destroy every representation I might make, by saying 'If there had been anything wrong Holyoake would have complained, but as he has not done so, the aggravation he points out could not have existed, or could not have been grievous.' Foreseeing this I provided against it, and disregarding the refusal of my applications, I addressed them all round with scrupulous formality. The result was, that on my liberation I found myself in a position to defy contradiction in any allegations I had to advance; and though I published this letter immediately under the eyes of the magistrates, it was never contradicted.

* In consequence of these representations some medical gentlemen of the city were brought in to examine me, who pronounced my life to be in no danger, and therefore (so it seemed) my health was not regarded as worth improving by better food. Provided I did not make a case for the House of Commons, that was enough. They appeared to consider themselves as bound to keep me alive and no more.

surgeon I wish to speak impartially, and I gladly admit, that his manner was always very kind, but I complain that his answers were always very indecisive. What he recommended he seldom prescribed, and professed that he must consult the governor when he should have consulted only himself. This fault may seem little, but its effects are great. In a gaol, the surgeon is the only person who stands between a prisoner and the grave, and it is indispensable that to the quality of humanity those of independence and decision should be joined. The kind of answers to which I have alluded were given to me more than once, and given to others as well as to me. And I again repeat, that had I been without friends, I should have left my prison without health.

'Akin to the want of better food, was the want of exercise, and *no* want of damp. The yard in which I walked was so small, that I always became giddy, through the frequent turnings, before I became refreshed. The governor sometimes permitted the "Fines-Class" in which I was, to walk in his garden; but the occasions came seldom and lasted not long—and I was previously so enervated by confinement, that the unusual exercise thus taken, threw me into a slight fever. Generally speaking, the place in which I was confined was miserably humid, and, although I took perpetual care, I had almost a perpetual cold.

'An application for a trivial favour often brought down upon me ruthless treatment. The visiting magistrates would come, and before the other prisoners denounce me as the " worst felon in the gaol, and the most atrocious of criminals." I was directed to ascribe this to the petulance of age and the rancour of orthodoxy; but I thought it proceeded from bad taste and worse feeling.

'From first to last, every newspaper sent me was detained; every letter *from* me was perused, and every one *to* me was broken open and read—and the very seals, if they happened to be heterodox, were interdicted. Thus the privacy of affection and friendship were violated, and mind as well as body laid under one restraint.

'When I saw friends it was but for a few minutes, and then through the bars of a gate; to shake hands was a privilege, and to converse unheard, impossible. To me it was a momentary satisfaction made an enduring mortification. To the public it may seem a light matter that nothing can be spoken to a visitor unheard by officers, but it is no light matter to a prisoner. The commissioners inquired—" Can you make *no* communication to your friends without its passing under the eyes of the governor, or through the ears of the turnkey ?" I answered—" *None;* and that it was not prudent for a prisoner to mention openly what affected persons in whose power he was put—that no prisoner must calculate on gaolers being generous, for they owned few virtues not written in their rules." I spoke from experience, and gave them cases in point.*

'During the latter portion of my time all my friends were denied access to me,† which, though it interfered with the supply of my wants, I did not, for the reasons stated, much regret. But this I did regret—all my letters were detained, and I was refused the privilege of writing a single letter to my family. The reason assigned by the governor for this was the enforcement of new rules, but I know that they were enforced without proper authority, and I believe applied only to me.‡

'Those are happy who are for ever preserved from the reception cells of Gloucester Gaol. Of the one in which I was put, the floor was filthy, the bed was filthier, and the window was filthier still, for in the window was—what I sicken at while I write—a rag full of human excrement. And of the bed, a prisoner assured me that when he lay in it the lice crept up his throat off the corners of the blanket which covered him. This statement, on my direction, he made to the commissioners.

'The gaol chapel is a cold place. Often, on entering it, I have exclaimed, with Jugurtha, on entering his Roman dungeon—"Heavens! how cold is this bath of yours!" Yet in this place, during this inclement season, the prisoners are assembled every morning to hear prayers, on empty stomachs, after sixteen hours' confinement in their night cells. On the "long prayer" mornings, they are detained in chapel three-quarters of an hour, and the penitentiary men, on their return to their cells, find their gruel on the stone floor, gone cold in their absence. I mention this matter with reluctance, as some may suppose that I notice it only from want of religion; but perhaps a little reflection will convince them that believers, as well as unbelievers, can appre-

---

* One case I allude to was this. Mr. Bransby Cooper and Mr. Jones had called me out to state that an application I had made for better dietary would not be acceded to. Mr. Cooper said the surgeon did not prescribe any other diet. I said, 'It appears to me, sir, that the surgeon *dare not* prescribe any other diet, unless he was first assured you would approve of it.' The answer of Mr. Cooper was loud, harsh, brief, and decisive.' Of course, sir, he dare not.' Thus the fierce candour of this man broke through the webwork of cautiousness which surrounded prisoners there, and spoke the truth for once.

† I have since been told that Mr. Alcott, of America, was among the number, who, being a visitor in England, had but one opportunity of calling upon me.

‡ On one occasion Richard Carlile brought me a present of a handsome pair of large razors, which were sent back lest I should cut my throat with them. The rules of the gaol forbid the entrance of such articles, but this reason for their rejection was not in the rules, but added as suitable to my case.

ciate a warm breakfast on a cold morning!—and that an asthmatical man, however sound his faith, will have his affection painfully increased by enervation, inanition, and sudden cold. This practice I do not say is contrary to the rules, for it would be difficult to say what is, or what is not, contrary to them—and I never met with any one at the gaol who could tell. But the practice is contrary to the act of the 4th of Geo. IV., chap. 64, sec. 30, which is professed to regulate it.

'A circumstance of a different nature from any of the foregoing I think it my duty to notice. After a considerable portion of my term of imprisonment had elapsed, and after I had memorialised Sir James Graham, I was permitted to remain up in an evening with my books. To this I owe what of pleasure I can be said to have experienced in gaol, and with pleasure I acknowledge it.*

'I prefer leaving these statements without comment, and content myself with saying, that I can abundantly substantiate every one of them. On Saturday last they were partly examined at the gaol by the magistrates, but I heard nothing that impugned their correctness or affected the propriety of their appearing before the public. If I have made any misrepresentations, I shall be sorry; and what is *proved* to be wrong I will cheerfully retract. I have written from no malevolence, for I feel none, and, as what I have related affects me no longer, my only motive is the hope of benefiting the unfortunate beings whom I have left behind me. My object is not, as some may suspect, to excite commiseration on my own part; to do this I have no wish, and no expectation, for in Cheltenham it seems to be a received maxim, that they who have little faith have no feelings —certainly, none are respected.

'How my imprisonment is supposed to affect me toward religion, I cannot tell; I only know that I have no change of sentiment to own. During six months I have been " shut out from the common light and common air "—from those whom the bonds of friendship connected, and the ties of affection endeared; and some of these ties are broken for ever. After this, I can only

---

* Before this privilege was conceded I whiled away the long nights by writing on the cover of a book, on which I had adjusted threads at equal intervals; under these threads I slipped paper, and thus wrote on the lines made by the threads, which kept in the dark the words from running into each other. When a boy I learned to write with my eyes shut, and my playful acquirement now became of service to me. In this way I wrote some letters for the *Oracle*, and much of my correspondence. Scattered by force, our little party at that time, and for some years after, had to be kept together by letters, and, incredible as it will sound, I wrote during my imprisonment from first to last nearly 2000 letters. The governor did not see them all, but he saw so many, that one day he said I sent out more letters than usually went through a local post office.

say, that I have greater difficulty than ever in believing that humanity is the associate of piety; and if Christianity has no expounders more attractive than those I have fallen in with, the day of my conversion is still distant.

'It was taught to me that the religion of Jesus cherished kindness, that it promoted our best affections, and reclaimed the erring in love. But how is this accomplished in gaol? The man who goes there must leave his affections, his feelings, and his sensibilities behind him—for in gaol all are blighted, deadened, and destroyed. *There* no appeals are made but to coward fears, and no antidote applied to error but misery. Indeed, I cannot dwell upon Christianity's treatment of what she considers my errors, without wishing, with Themistocles, that I could learn the art of forgetting. With regard to the cause of my prosecution, I admit that I might be wrong in the sentiments which I held, but I could not be wrong in frankly avowing them. And I may answer to Christians, as did Aristides to the tyrant Dionysius—"I am sorry for what you have done, but I am not sorry for what I have said." Despite all that has succeeded, I still prefer integrity to liberty. My resolution has long been taken, to speak nothing or to speak what I think—for

> Who dares think one thing and another tell,
> My heart detests him as the gates of hell.

'Christians speak what they think useful, and the same privilege ought to be conceded to me. A difference in faith ought not to make a difference in right. But while it does so, those who cannot pronounce the required Shibboleth must arm themselves to bear. Those are poor principles for which a man is unwilling to suffer when they are in danger. It is an encouraging reflection, that though a man's fate may be at others' disposal, his character is ever at his own—and that no enemy can dishonour him who will not dishonour himself.

'Yours respectfully,
'Gloucester, Feb. 7, 1843.   G. J. HOLYOAKE.'

The Commissioners referred to in this letter asked me, when I was first taken before them, whether I had any complaint to make?

I said I had.

Did I wish to give it as evidence?

I said I did.

In the evening of the next day, between 9 and 10 o'clock, I was called up and taken into their presence again. The governor of the gaol, Captain Mason, and the surgeon, Mr. Hicks, were present.

'Take a seat, Mr. Holyoake,' said the speaker of the Board—Dr. Blissett Hawkins, I believe.

I did so.

'Now, Mr. Holyoake, what have you to complain of?' said the speaking Commissioner.

'Nothing, sir.'

'Nothing! Why what do you mean?'

'What I say, sir.'

'But did you not say that you had evidence that you wished to give?'

'I did.'

'Has it not been at your request that you have been brought before us for that purpose?'

'It has.'

'Then what are we to understand by your present statement?'

'Why, sir, what you hardly need me to explain. I cannot give evidence before these gentlemen,' looking towards the governor and the surgeon.

'True,' said the questioner. 'Captain Mason, Mr. Hicks, you will please to withdraw.'

When they were gone, 'Now, Mr. Holyoake, you can speak freely,' said the chairman.

'But first I must have your guarantee that I shall suffer no inconvenience in consequence.'

'Why what danger do you run?' was asked me.

'This. Am I not in the power of governor and surgeon? Can they not retaliate in your absence? No prisoner is safe in any gaol, as you ought to know, if the authorities come to regard him as reporting them. If you decline to give me this guarantee I shall not make any communication to you, and when I am at liberty again, I shall have a right to publish that your commission did not learn the whole truth at this gaol—that it did not even put itself in a condition to learn it.'

'Well,' the chairman said, 'We guarantee that you shall suffer no inconvenience in consequence of any evidence you may give to us.'

Then, and not till then, did I proceed to explain what in the last letter and notes is recounted. The commissioners kept their word. The severity of the discipline, instituted by the governor when a visitor came, was somewhat relaxed; and once or twice, when I was suffering from cold (before unnoticed), a can of mutton broth was ordered me by the surgeon, in which I found a very sensible looking piece of mutton.

Nothing more of importance remains to be narrated. Concluding, let me solicit consideration to the moral aspects of Christianity, as set forth in this narrative, and to what I consider the political moral of these pages. Many persons whose candour and general intelligence I do not distrust, tell me that the persecution here recounted, is not to be ascribed to Christianity. To this I make the answer made on this subject (the imprisonment of myself, Adams, and others) by my late friend, Maltus Questell Ryall. 'Christians set a watch upon them—Christians informed against them—Christians prejudiced the public against them: by Christian pay were hireling lawyers retained—by Christian witnesses confronted—by the Christian Press misrepresented—by Christian juries found guilty, by Christian judges condemned.' It is necessary to put the argument in this cumulative form to satisfy some understandings; but a well-informed and candid Christian can hardly be supposed to need formal proof on this head. A careful study of the Evangelists some time after this imprisonment, satisfied me that the religion of Jesus involves persecution. A man who believes that men need saving, that there is only one way whereby they can be saved, that *his* way is that way, and that it is better for a man to lose the whole world than to lose his own soul by missing that way, such a believer will inevitably coerce all he can into it. If he is not a persecutor he ought, in moral consistency, to be one. Having the fear of the philanthropists and of the humanitarians before his eyes, he may modify his practice, but it will be at the expense of his penetration or of his religious duty. I have no difficulty whatever in understanding that the conscientious among the old inquisitors might be men of benevolence—spiritual physicians, who amputated existence with a view to save the eternal life of the patient. It is now many years since I wrote or spoke against them on religious grounds, and for a long period I have ceased to speak of persecution as being either unscriptural or unchristian.

It will not do to say that what we have seen of persecution has been but the abuse of Christianity. It is in itself a condemnation of Christianity to be obliged to repudiate the conduct of all Christian churches. It will not do to say that Christians have not been wise enough to see, nor good enough to image, the divine gentleness of Christ. The Christian churches have been presided over by pastors who have possessed both penetration and purity in the highest degree—who were able to see what there was to be seen, and devout enough to render it in their lives. Try the question even in our day. If Christ be the symbol of love and gentleness to all who believe in his name, how is it that in every part of the world the Freethinker should fear to fall into the hands of the Christian? How is it that he must set a watch upon his words in every town and hamlet in our own land, lest the free expression of his deepest convictions should cost him his position, his employment, and his character? Branded, outcast, and friendless, the Christian's door is the last at which he would knock—the Christian's fireside is the last at which he would find a welcome—and the Christian pastor, who in knowledge, duty, and example, most nearly resembles the Christ whom he preaches, is the last man whose path the Freethinker would wish to cross, or into whose ear he would venture to pour the tale of his expatriations.

In one passage in my defence I represent persecution, as Lord Brougham and others have done, as a power which *spreads* opinion. I believed so then, but believe it no longer. I have lived to watch the effects of persecution, and have seen it *put down* the *truth* so often, as no longer to doubt its bad efficacy. The ignorant, the timid, the opulent, and the conventional (and these make up the mass of mankind), are all deterred by danger or opprobrium. The resolute and the reckless, the only parties who persist, labour under accumulated disadvantages. Condemned to spend their time in self-defence, development of doctrine—the legitimate and only source of permanent influence—is nearly impossible to them: and it is well for them if they escape acquiring an antagonistic spirit, which disfigures their advocacy and misrepresents their character. Their only proselytes are those who come to them out of spite or out of sympathy, and who of course miss the intellectual ground of conviction, and can be of little real service until they have been re-educated.

If, as I admit, persecution *will* put down opinion, what objection, is there to its employment when it puts down error? I answer, 'Beware of its use, because it may put down the *truth* also.' Persecution is not an ordeal. Free discussion is the only test capable of distinguishing and establishing the truth. The proper condemnation of persecution is, that it is an illegitimate opposition which is sure to be discountenanced as men become manly and refined. The armies of a civilised people observe, even in the deadly strife of battle, some rules of honourable warfare, and do not descend to the arts of treachery or tactics of savages. We may surely hope that in the battle for religious truth, a sense of honour will prevent the dominant party from taking against its opponents the undue advantage of persecution. Montaigne relates that when Polyperchon advised Alexander to take advantage of the night for attacking Darius, ' By no means,' answered the noble general; ' It is not for such a man as I am to steal such an advantage; *I had rather repent me of my fortune than be ashamed of my victory.*' It is not too much to expect that Christianity will always be less refined than War.

Persecution, always a disaster, was not however with us a defeat. We were not put down by persecution; we continued the *Oracle* a hundred and four weeks, then the *Movement*, sixty-eight weeks, and the *Reasoner* will soon have completed ten volumes. Besides having written in our publications, we have, in almost all the principal cities and towns in the kingdom, spoken, since the trial at Gloucester, with the utmost explicitness. The imprisonment has at least been of this service—and this is all—it has enabled me to speak accredited by the sincerity which otherwise could not have been so satisfactorily manifest to the multitude. To have spent, without shrinking, some portion of life in prison in defence of public liberty, gives the same authority among the people as having graduated at a university does among scholars.* The fact is a sad illustration of the brutal manner in which the people are condemned to win the enlargement of their liberties. In cases where clergymen have menaced me with renewed imprisonment, I have always answered—' I consider myself as having taken out a license to speak freely. The government made a charge to me of six months' imprisonment for that privilege, and I paid the price. If you have renewed demands upon me, let me know them, and I will endeavour to meet them; but do not interrupt me.'

In the present structure of English political society, to preserve the ability to be imprisoned is necessary to usefulness. When the associations of home have twined themselves around the feelings—after long industry and patient frugality have surrounded a man with some comforts unknown to his youth—few have the temper which will part from them and walk into a gaol at the call of duty. I should think this state the death of progress. When, some time ago, insuring my life in the Equity Law Insurance Office, I asked, before I took out my policy, whether it would be forfeited if my death was occasioned by imprisonment or transportation. The Directors naturally asked whether I was liable to those casualties. I said, not particularly liable I hoped; but to be able to be imprisoned, if it seemed a duty, I valued as a great privilege, and I would not barter my right to be imprisoned. I am afraid they smiled at my eccentricity, but they assured me that that accident would not involve the forfeiture of my policy—which I then took out.

No one who reads thus far will, I hope, consider me as a can-

* When the Prizes were awarded me for writing the Literary Lectures of the Manchester Unity, an attempt was made to cancel the award on the ground of my having been imprisoned, but it was immediately quashed. When the legislation of the Order was before the House of Lords, the Bishop of Oxford (in Committee) made an objection to the Lectures on account of the Authorship, but the Unity refused to withdraw them, and they are in use to this day. The objections of this nature made in some instances by the Press have been inoperative where the people have been concerned.

didate for either imprisonment or transportation. I have too keen an insight into their misery for that. But he who pretends to take the side of the people ought to see his way *all through*, and not incur a danger he has not weighed, and not suffer any to ascribe to him a virtue he does not mean to maintain.

If any, from what I have just expressed, or from the transactions of this narrative, shall conclude that I am disposed to regard law-breaking lightly, they will mistake me. Respect for the law is an intelligent virtue — a sign of fitness for freedom so important that none but an enemy would obscure the duty or weaken the sentiment. If accused, in the matter which led to my Trial, of breaking the law, I might plead that there was no law to break, and therefore I could not break one. What is called the common law relating to blasphemy is a mere caprice, an opinion interpreted by ignorance or sectarian prejudice, and enforced at the call of bigotry—malevolent to the humble while neutral towards the rich. Against this tyranny one is obliged to rebel. It is disastrous that we should have to set up the standard of resistance even in a case of this kind, and the chief justification is that a democratic government is denied us. Had the people a voice in making the laws, the breaking of any law would require grave justification. Men have two lives—a private and a public one. Conscience is the guide of all that relates to private duty, but law is the conscience of society, and it is best when private conscience can be subordinate to the public conscience. Private conscience *may* be the child of selfishness, fanaticism, or vanity, as well as of the greatest purity and intelligence. A man, therefore, should be careful how he places so uncertain a thing above the law. If private conscience be more just and intelligent than the public conscience, a democratic form of government affords peaceful facilities whereby it can come into the ascendant. But where these modes are denied, no alternative remains but that of rebellion or unconditional and indefinite submission. Resistance to the law, however, or to what is tacitly accepted by the majority as law, is, under any form of government, so pernicious an example, is so liable to be abused, so liable to unfit the people who learn the lesson, for submission to legitimate authority, that these cases demand the strictest surveillance before they receive the sanction of a friend of the people. In all instances in which conscience is the ground of resistance, the wrong done to conscience ought to be clear, deep, and momentous, and the necessity which obliges the claims of private conscience to be put above the laws ought to be made so evident that the sentiment of freedom shall not deteriorate that of legitimate and honourable allegiance

If the political moral of this narrative be therefore drawn with discrimination, we may do little harm even if mistaken in the belief that the prevalence of our views of life may be a public good; and if this belief prove to be right in the main, we do what reformers are said often to forget—we make a past to which the future may refer for authority and instruction.

> Then not 'in vain!' Even obscurest weeds
> Nourish the roots of fruitfulest fair trees
> So from our Fortune-loathed Hope proceeds
> The experience that may base high victories.*

What 'our views' are this is not the place to state; as to some it would seem that under the pretext of a plea for Free Utterance, sentiments were obtruded upon the reader he was not forewarned to expect. I therefore limit myself to saying (and that only for the sake of others who will decline to concede free utterance until they know what has to be uttered) that whoever sees in Atheism simply the development of a *negation*, sees but half the truth. Even in this respect (supposing existing theological systems to be erroneous) Atheism has the merit of clearing the way for Pure Moralism—which is the other half, or *positive* ground of Atheism. The latest writers on the Philosophy of Religion resolve religion into *Dependance*; by which its modern theory at length coincides with its ancient practice. We venture to think that this is not salutary teaching. Life should be self-reliant. It seems to us that the light of Nature and the experience of man are anterior to the dogmas of Priests, and are the sources whence guidance and duty independently spring. The Priest breaks in upon the integrity of life, and diverts its course. He says he makes an addition to our knowledge—we do not find it so. He professes to show us the hidden mysteries of the future —we fail to see them. He simply encumbers us, and we pray him to stand aside. The responsibility of our course is our own and not his, and we have a right to be left free. Rejecting his advices, he proclaims that we reject truth, honour, justice, love. This is his error or the retaliation of his disappointment. We appeal to the candid and the impartial to judge between us. We respect Theology as the science of man's destiny, and regret that it bears no fruits for us: but this is not our fault; and we therefore attempt to solve the problem of life for ourselves. Our progress already counts some distinct steps. We have recast the practice of controversy: we forbid to ourselves to suspect evil motives, or to impute insincerity to others; the doubtful act we propose to judge by evidence alone, and to put the best construction on the dubious word. Thus we annihilate Antagonism, the

* W. J. Linton.

eldest foe of Progress, by imposing laws on impulse. Our search in every system is directed after *moral truth;* and, less exacting than the Christian, we accept it, whether given by Inspiration, confirmed by Miracle, attested by Prophecy, or not. Probity of word and act may be securely based on the intelligence and refinement of mankind—and this we labour to enforce. To restrict human expectation to that which is ascertainable by reason, must have the effect of concentrating attention on humanity, and intensifying interest in human exertions. In Solidarity we find the encouragement to public endeavour, and we sum up private duty in Honour, which is respecting the Truth; in Morality, which is acting the Truth; and in Love, which is serving the Truth.

THE **END**.

THE ATHEIST VIEWPOINT

AN ARNO PRESS / NEW YORK TIMES COLLECTION

Amberley, [John Russell], Viscount. **An Analysis of Religious Belief.** 1877.

Atheist Magazines: A Sampling, 1927–1970. New Introduction by Madalyn Murray O'Hair. 1972.

Besant, Annie. **The Freethinker's Text-Book:** Part II—Christianity. n.d.

[Burr, William Henry.] **Revelations of Antichrist.** 1879.

Cardiff, Ira D. **What Great Men Think of Religion.** 1945.

Champion of Liberty: Charles Bradlaugh. 1934.

Cohen, Chapman. **Primitive Survivals in Modern Thought.** 1935.

Drews, Arthur. **The Witnesses to the Historicity of Jesus.** Translated by Joseph McCabe. 1912.

Ferrer [y Guardia], Francisco. **The Origins and Ideals of the Modern School.** Translated by Joseph McCabe. 1913.

Foote, G. W. and W. P. Ball, editors. **The Bible Handbook.** 1961.

Gibbon, Edward. **History of Christianity.** 1883.

Holyoake, George Jacob. **The History of the Last Trial by Jury for Atheism in England.** 1851.

Komroff, Manuel, editor. **The Apocrypha or Non-Canonical Books of the Bible:** The King James Version. 1936.

Lewis, Joseph. **Atheism and Other Addresses.** 1960.

McCarthy, William. **Bible, Church and God.** 1946.

Macdonald, George E. **Fifty Years of Freethought.** 1929, 1931. Two volumes in one.

Manhattan, Avro. **Catholic Imperialism and World Freedom.** 1952.

Meslier, Jean. **Superstition in All Ages.** Translated from the French original by Anna Knoop. 1890.

Nietzsche, Friedrich. **The Antichrist.** 1930.

O'Hair, Madalyn Murray. **What on Earth Is an Atheist!** 1969.

Robertson, J. M. **A Short History of Freethought.** 1957.

Russell, Bertrand. **Atheism: Collected Essays, 1943–1949.** 1972.

Shelley, Percy Bysshe. **Selected Essays on Atheism.** (n.d.) 1972.

Teller, Woolsey. **The Atheism of Astronomy.** 1938.

Wells, H. G. **Crux Ansata:** An Indictment of the Roman Catholic Church. 1944.

DATE DUE

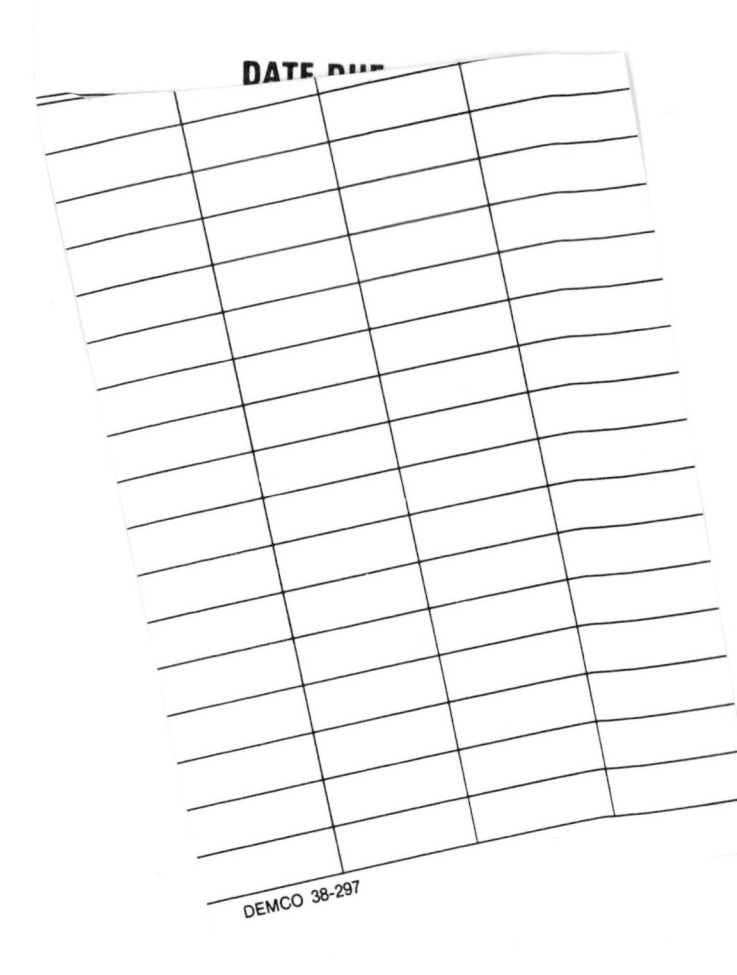

DEMCO 38-297

DE PAUL UNIVERSITY LIBRARY

30511000080733

345.42H761H C001
LPX THE HISTORY OF THE LAST TRIAL BY JU